Technical Drawing with AutoCAD

Jeff Hung

Farmingdale State College

LINUS
Learning

Published by Linus Learning
Deer Park, NY 11729

ISBN 10: 1-60797-434-7

ISBN 13: 978-1-60797-434-5

Printed in the United States of America.

Print Numbers   5   4   3   2   1

TABLE OF CONTENTS

Acknowledgment vii

CHAPTER 1

Introduction to Technical Drawing 1

1.1 Title block...2

1.2 Border...2

1.3 Line Types, Symbols and Abbreviation 3

1.4 Drawing scales...5

1.5 Standard US Engineering Drawing sizes...7

CHAPTER 2

Orthographic Projection...9

2.1 Line type applications...12

2.2 Inclined planes and curved surfaces 13

2.3 General steps to construct drawings with orthographic views 14

2.4 Important rules for orthographic projections 17

    2.4.1 Examples of correct and incorrect orthographic projections 18

CHAPTER 3

Dimensioning and Tolerancing..33

3.1 Types of dimensions and techniques...33

3.2 Dimensioning specifications...36

3.3 Rules and practices...37

3.4 Tolerancing 37

    3.4.1 Types of fit 38

    3.4.2 Types of tolerance 38

    3.4.3 Tolerance Accumulation 39

CHAPTER 4

Additional views 41

4.1 Sectional views..41

    4.1.1 Construction of sectional views...41

4.1.2 Line types used in sectional views..42

4.1.3 Types of sectional views 42

4.2 Detail views...46

4.3 Broken views 47

4.4 Auxiliary views...48

CHAPTER 5

Pictorial sketching (Isometric view)
....53

5.1 Basic concept of isometric drawings...53

5.2 Tangent edges 60

CHAPTER 6

Introduction to AutoCAD (ACAD)
....63

6.1 Workspaces...63

6.2 User Interface 64

6.3 Methods of commanding 64

6.3.1 Ribbon 64

6.3.2 Command Line Window..65

6.3.3 Graphics Window..65

6.4 Controlling and Viewing..66

6.5 AutoCAD Basics 67

6.5.1 Sign conventions..67

6.5.2 Angel convention 67

6.5.3 Absolute and relative coordinates systems 68

CHAPTER 7

Drawing Setups and Plotting
....71

7.1 Drawing units..71

7.1.1 How to setup drawing units for drawings.....................................71

7.2 Drawing limits...72

7.2.1 Functions of drawing limits 72

7.2.2 How to turn drawing limits on or off 72

7.2.3 How to set drawing limits...73

7.3 Title block..73

7.3.1 Model 73

7.3.2 Layout...73

7.3.3 The general procedures to setup a title block in a drawing 74

7.4 Plotting 77

7.4.1 How to print drawings 78

CHAPTER 8

Draw and Text Commands 81

8.1 Types of Draw and Text Commands 81

8.2 Orthogonal locking 83

8.3 Special section: Important notes for the lessons 83

Lesson 1. 84

Lesson 2. 87

Lesson 3. 91

Lesson 4. 94

CHAPTER 9

Object Snaps 99

9.1 Types of object snaps and their functions. 100

9.1.1 How to setup and apply Object Snaps 101

9.2 Selection techniques 102

9.3 Grid Display 103

9.3.1 How to adjust grid display 104

Lesson 5 – Part 1 105

Lesson 5 – Part 2 (Selection techniques) 111

Lesson 6. 112

CHAPTER 10

Modify Commands 119

10.1 Types of Modify commands 119

Lesson 7. 121

Lesson 8. 124

Lesson 9. 129

CHAPTER 11

Dimensioning and Tolerancing in AutoCAD 139

11.1 Editing Dimension Style 140

11.1.1 How to edit the current Dimension Style 141

11.1.2 How to create new Dimension Style..144

Lesson 10 145

CHAPTER 12

Line types and Layers 151

12.1 Linetypes and colors...151

12.1.1 How to change the linetype of an existing object(s) 151

12.2 Layers...153

12.2.1 Layer command and its functions 153

12.2.2 How to assign an object(s) into a different layer 154

12.3 Properties 155

12.3.1 How to assign different properties to an object(s)...156

ACKNOWLEDGMENTS

I would like to take this opportunity to thank my professors, Prof. Hazem Tawfik, Prof. Serdar Elgun, Prof. Mahendra Shah, Prof. Dimitrios Maltezos, Prof. Ahmed Ibrahim, Prof. Leon Taub, and the former Chairperson Prof. John Tiedemann from the Mechanical Engineering Technology (MET) department at Farmingdale State College. They have been a great support and excellent advisors since I was a student of theirs. Everything I learned from them has had a positive impact on my life.

A special thanks to Prof. Hazem Tawfik who introduced me to the basics of computer aided design; I owe him special thanks for directing me through my Bachelor's, Master's, and Doctoral degrees as well as for reviewing this book. Also, a special thanks to my colleague Daniel Weinman for reviewing this book as well.

INTRODUCTION TO TECHNICAL DRAWING

Drawing is essential in every engineering field. It is one of the important communication tools between engineers. It provides a basic guideline for any design ideas and it also acts like a small but extremely useful contract between the designer and manufacturer. Engineers must be able to create, read, and understand technical drawings because they need the drawings to convey their design and technical ideas to each other. For example, Architects document their design ideas on drawings so that civil engineers can follow the specifications of the designs when they are constructing a building. Mechanical engineers indicate all design specifications of products such as size, shape, and materials, in drawings so that manufacturing engineers are able to produce these products accordingly.

Moreover, almost everything we use nowadays is mass produced, such as televisions, phones, cars, airplanes, glasses, milk bottles, and more. These products have their own design specifications. Engineers are required to create drawings with design specifications for these products before they are mass produced. Therefore, technical drawing is often the first introductory course for engineering students. The drafting techniques introduced in this book mainly focus on mechanical engineering applications. Figure 1.1 shows an example of a technical drawing with a sheet layout which includes a **title block**, a **border** and **drawing views** (with different types of lines and dimensions).

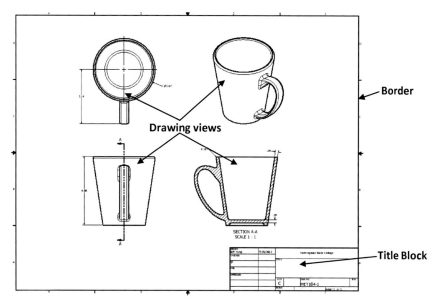

FIGURE 1.1: An example of a technical drawing

1.1 TITLE BLOCK

Title Block style does not have a fixed layout. Figure 1.2 shows an example of a title block. It depends on companies or individuals but it normally includes the following items:

» Designer's /Engineer's Name

» Company name

» Date

» Drawing number

» Drawing Title

» Scales

» Revision number

» General tolerance

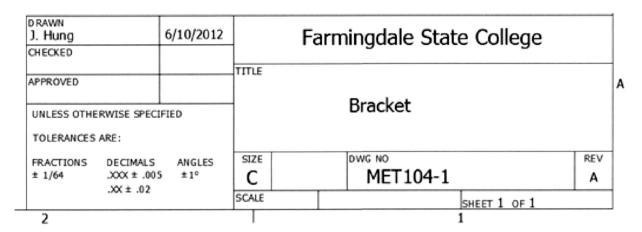

FIGURE 1.2: An example of a title block

1.2 BORDER

The border of a drawing typically contains numerical and alphabetical divisions. These divisions provide a great mapping system for users to reference their drawings. Figure 1.3 shows how the numerical and alphabetical divisions are used in the drawing. The location of dimensions or other information can be clearly identified by indicating the divisions. For example, the dimension located in the left of the top view can be easily identified by the divisions of C-4 as shown in Figure 1.3.

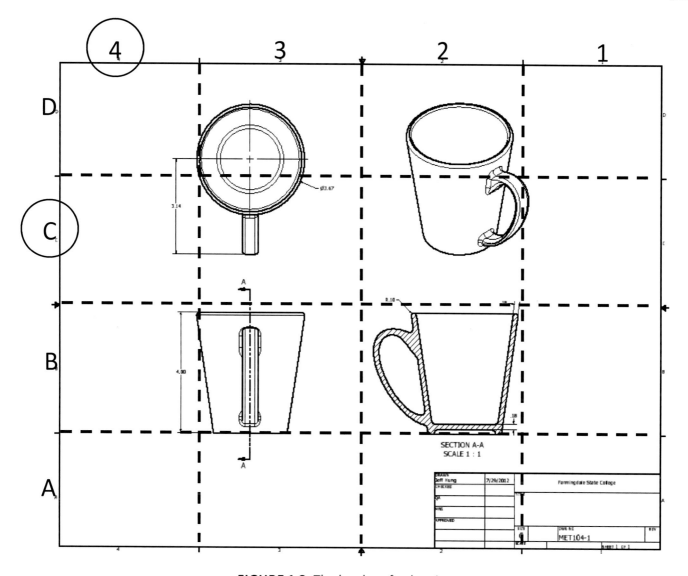

FIGURE 1.3: The border of a drawing

1.3 LINE TYPES, SYMBOLS AND ABBREVIATION

Drawing views show all the information about an object such as size and shape. These views may contain different types of lines, symbols, and abbreviations. Each of these items has its own function and meaning within the drawing views. Table 1.1 shows the line types and their functions and Table 1.2 shows the commonly used symbols and abbreviations.

In the case of lines overlapping or coinciding, the priority of lines is in the following order:

1.   Visible lines
2.   Hidden lines
3.   Cutting plan lines
4.   Centerlines

TABLE 1.1: Line types and their functions

Line types	Function and Recommended Specifications
Visible Line ————————	Use for visible edges of an object. Thickness: **0.024″ (0.6mm)**
Construction Line ————————	Temporary lines (Should be removed after the drawing is completed). Thickness: **0.012″ (0.3mm)**
Hidden Line – – – – – – – – –	Use for invisible edges of an object. Thickness: **0.012″ (0.3mm)** Size: ⊢ 0.12″ (3.0mm) ⊣ ⊢ 0.03″ (0.8mm) ⊣
Centerline — – — – — – —	Use for indicating the symmetry of an object. (e.g. tube, slots, and holes) Thickness: **0.012″ (0.3mm)** Size: 0.75″-1.50″ (19-38mm) / 0.06″ (1.5mm) / 0.12″ (3.0mm)
Phantom Line — – – — – – —	Use for imaginary features. Thickness: **0.012″ (0.3mm)** Size: 0.75″-1.50″ (19-38mm) / 0.06″ (1.5mm) / 0.12″ (3.0mm)
Cutting Plane Line ↑└ – – — – – ┘↑	Use for indicating the location of an imaginary cutting plane. Thickness: **0.024″ (0.6mm)** Size: 0.75″-1.50″ (19-38mm) / 0.06″ (1.5mm) / 0.12″ (3.0mm)
Section Line ////////// (A group of equally spaced and parallel lines)	Use for showing an object that is cut by the imaginary cutting plane. Thickness: **0.012″ (0.3mm)** Angle: 30°, 45°, and 60° Spacing: Minimum of 0.06″ (1.5mm)
Dimension Line ⊢—— 3.00 ——⊣ (Consists of extension lines, arrows, and a number)	Use for showing dimensions of an object. Thickness: **0.012″ (0.3mm)** Size: (See chapter 3 for more details)

TABLE 1.2: Symbols and their functions

Symbols and Abbreviations	Examples	Descriptions
R	R1.5	Radius of 1.5″
Ø	Ø2.5	Diameter of 2.5″
TYP	Ø2.5 TYP	Typical: Diameter of 2.5″ for all circles that are not specified
THRU	Ø 0.25 THRU	0.25″ diameter through hole
⊔, ▼	⊔ Ø0.5▼0.75	0.5″ diameter counterbore with the depth of 0.75″
2X, 4X or 6X…etc	2 X R1.5	Radius of 1.5″ in two places
±	2.000 ± 0.005	Nominal dimension of 2″ with tolerance between 1.995″ and 2.005″ (For tolerance use)

1.4 DRAWING SCALES

For many Computer Aided Drafting (CAD) applications, it is a common practice to scale projected views up or down to fit drawing sheets properly. However, drawing views must be scaled up or down together using the same scales for consistency. Randomly applying scales on different views can result in confusion to the readers. Examples of drawing scales are listed in Table 1.3. It is important to emphasize that dimension annotations should have no effect on drawing scales. For example, if applying a half scale on a 5″ long object in a drawing, the dimension annotation of that object must still be 5″ long even though the size of the object on the paper is 2.5″ long.

TABLE 1.3: Drawing scales

Drawing scales	Descriptions	Meaning
1 : 1	1 unit on paper = 1 unit on the object	Full scale
1 : 2	1 unit on paper = 2 unit on the object	Half scale
1 : 4	1 unit on paper = 4 unit on the object	Quarter scale
2 : 1	2 unit on paper = 1 unit on the object	Double scale
5 : 1	5 unit on paper = 1 unit on the object	Five times scale

In addition, the scale of line types may need to be adjusted according to the size of the object or the scale of the drawing for better overall drawing presentation. All types of lines should not be too thin or too thick and some types of lines should not be too dense or too coarse, which could cause confusion and difficulty to read. Figures 1.4a and 1.4b show examples of acceptable and unacceptable scaling for hidden lines, centerlines, section lines, and dimension lines.

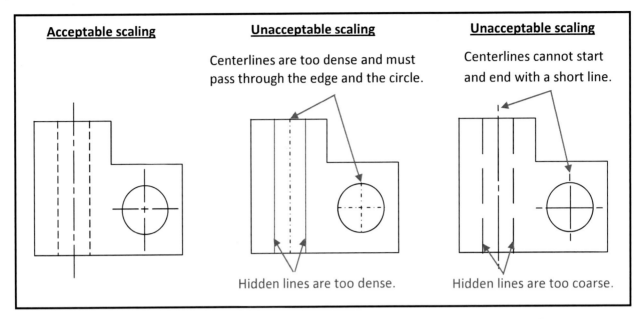

FIGURE 1.4A: Acceptable and unacceptable scaling for hidden lines and centerlines

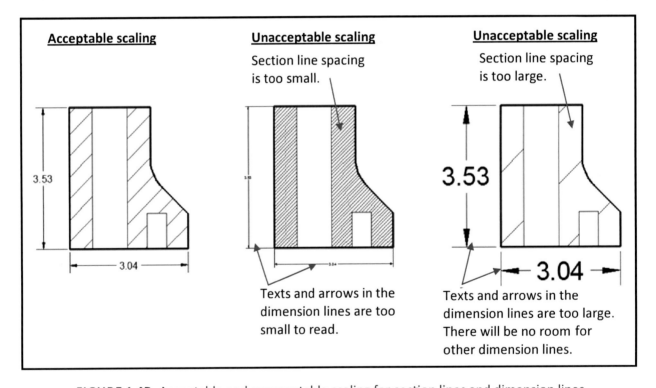

FIGURE 1.4B: Acceptable and unacceptable scaling for section lines and dimension lines

1.5 STANDARD US ENGINEERING DRAWING SIZES

American National Standards Institute (ANSI) standard paper sizes are one of the commonly used paper sizes in the United States. The dimensions and the relationship of paper sizes are listed and illustrated in Figure 1.5.

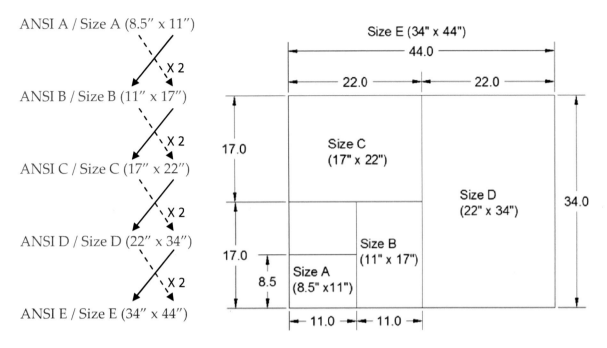

FIGURE 1.5: Dimensions and relationship of ANSI paper sizes

ORTHOGRAPHIC PROJECTION

Orthographic projection is the fundamental and effective technique to describe a 3D object on a 2D drawing. When the 2D drawing is constructed properly, engineers can quickly understand and retrieve information about the 3D object. The concept of orthographic projection can be imagined as a camera with X-ray capability taking front, side, top, and cross-sectional images of a 3D object. These images (views) can then be put together and organized to construct a meaningful 2D drawing. Two types of orthographic projection methods, namely, "First angle" and "Third angle" projections are used in the industry to arrange the projected views and they are distinguished by their symbols as shown in Figure 2.1a and 2.1b.

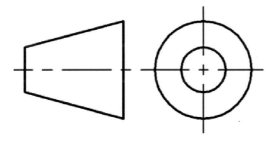

FIGURE 2.1a: First angle projection symbol

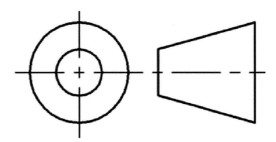

FIGURE 2.1b: Third angle projection symbol

These two projection methods can be explained by projecting images of a cone onto the walls of a clear box as shown in Figure 2.2. When the image is taken from the front direction, a trapezoid can be projected onto the front or the back plane of the box depending on the types of projection. To avoid confusion, for First angle projection, the trapezoid is **projected** onto the back plane (behind the object). For Third angle projection, the trapezoid is projected (**reflected**) onto the front plane (in front of the object) as demonstrated in Figure 2.2. Similarly, when the image is taken from the side direction using the Third angle projection, the image is projected onto the left side of the cone and onto the right side of the cone when using First angle projection. The arrangement of these images can represent the symbols of First angle and Third angle projections. Thus, by indicating the drawing with a proper symbol, readers can understand what type of projection method is used. In this book, all exercises and examples are created using the Third angle projection method which is widely used in the United States.

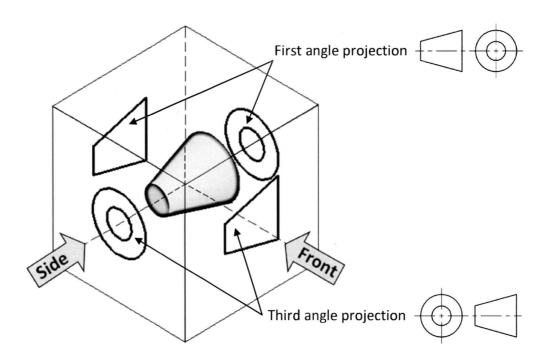

FIGURE 2.2: Difference between First and Third angle projections

In general, there are six principal views available for orthographic projections as shown in Figure 2.3. Keep in mind that it is not mandatory to use all six views to represent an object. The idea of using orthographic projections is to show all information about the object. If the front view showed all information about the object, it is not necessary to have the rear view. Depending on the complexity of the object, some objects may require only two views, and some may need all six views plus auxiliary views and sectional views (See chapter 4 for details about the additional views). Let us use the coffee cup as shown in Figure 2.4 as an example to create a 2D drawing. Using the clear box and the Third angle projection concepts discussed earlier, the outlines of the cup (images) are projected onto the top, bottom, left, right, front, and rear planes of the box. By unfolding the box, six projected views are lined up and arranged accordingly. This type of alignment and arrangement is extremely important. Mixing view locations will cause confusion to the readers. Figure 2.5 shows the proper 2D drawing of the coffee cup constructed using the Third angle orthographic projection method.

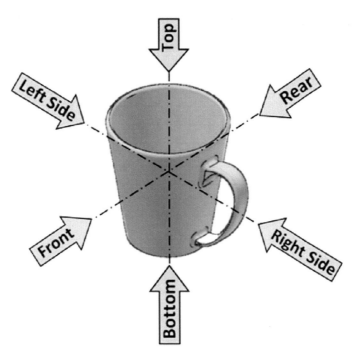

FIGURE 2.3: Six principal views of a 3D object

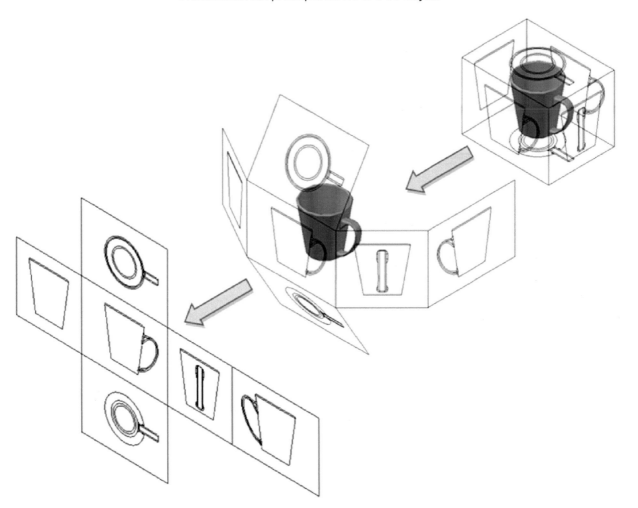

FIGURE 2.4: Concept of creating a 2D drawing using Third angle projection method

FIGURE 2.5: 2D drawing of a coffee cup

2.1 LINE TYPE APPLICATIONS

Although line types and their functions are explained in Chapter 1, it is worth discussing them again using an actual example as shown in Figure 2.6. The example includes the use of visible lines, hidden lines, and centerlines, which are the most frequently used line types in technical drawings.

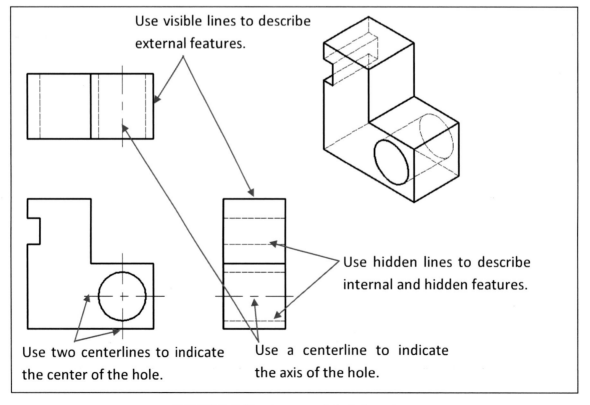

FIGURE 2.6: Line types and their functions

2.2 INCLINED PLANES AND CURVED SURFACES

In order to become proficient with orthographic projections, it is necessary to study some common mistakes in projection views, particularly in inclined planes and curved surfaces. Table 2.1 shows the correct and incorrect side views of vertical and horizontal planes, inclined planes, and curved surfaces.

TABLE 2.1: Common mistakes for inclined planes and curved surfaces

Isometric views	Front views	Side views	Common Side View Mistakes

2.3 GENERAL STEPS TO CONSTRUCT DRAWINGS WITH ORTHOGRAPHIC VIEWS

1. Evaluate the object and define the principal views for the object. (When defining the views, the object may be oriented in any position that is convenient for the engineer or to the paper orientation.)

2. Define the number of views necessary to present the object. (Additional views can always be added when necessary, defining the views earlier will allow proper spacing on the drawing sheet.)

3. The chosen views should show the essential contours and the shape of the object and should have the least number of hidden lines.

4. Define orthographic projection methods, First or Third. (This book introduces mainly the Third angle projection method.)

5. Construct the front view of the object.

6. Construct the remaining necessary views of the object.

Let us use the following example to demonstrate how to construct a 2D drawing from an object using Third angle projection method.

Example 2.1

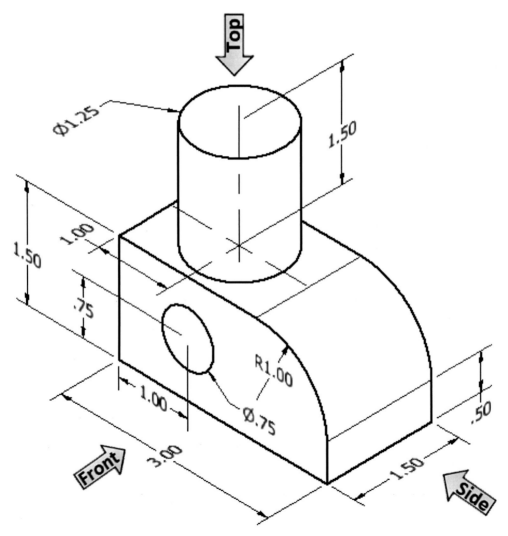

Steps

1   Construct the front view with all visible features of the object according to the given dimensions.

Create centerlines for cylindrical features.

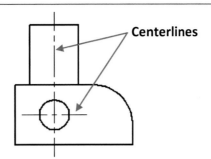

Centerlines

2   Create construction lines horizontally from the horizontal visible edges of the front view to the side view.

Since the height of both views is the same, the construction lines have defined the height of the side view.

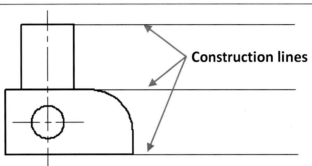

Construction lines

3   Construct the side view with proper widths (horizontal dimensions).

Create centerlines for cylindrical features.

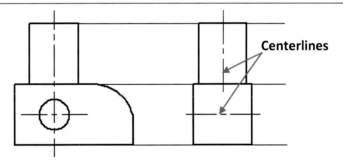

Centerlines

4   Create construction lines vertically from the vertical visible edges of the front view to the top view.

Since the length of both views is the same, the construction lines have defined the length of the top view.

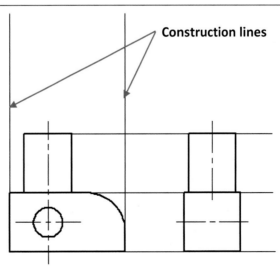

Construction lines

5 Create a 45° construction line from the upper right intersection of the most outward vertical and horizontal construction lines of the front view.

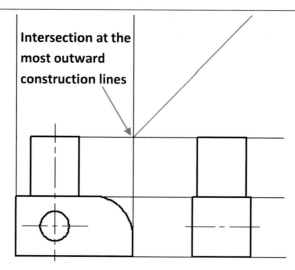

Intersection at the most outward construction lines

6 Create construction lines vertically from the vertical visible edges and the vertical centerline of the side view to the 45° construction line.

(Note: Construction lines from the side edges of the cylinder are not required.)

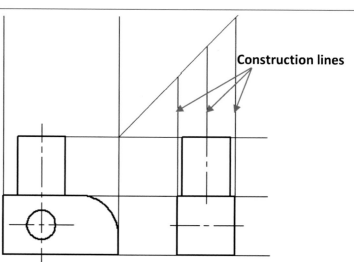

Construction lines

7 Create construction lines horizontally from the intersections along the 45° angled construction line to the top view.

Instead of measuring the vertical distance of the top view for each feature, the 45° construction line projects the width of the object from the side view to the top view.

Construct the top view by tracing the construction lines.

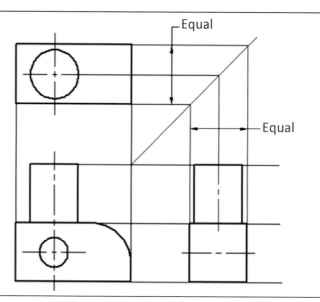

Equal

Equal

8   Hidden lines in the top and side views can be projected from the circle in the front view.

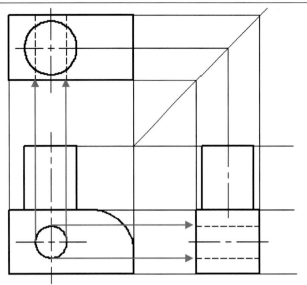

9   Remove the construction lines.

By starting the 45° construction line at the upper right intersection of the vertical and horizontal construction lines of the front view, the spacing between the views will be equal.

Note: It is also acceptable for unequal spacing between views due to limited space in the sheet layout.

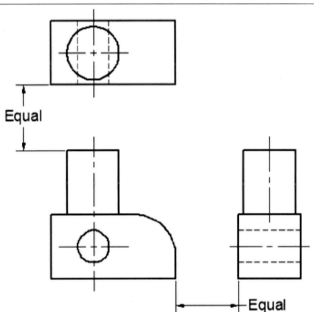

2.4 IMPORTANT RULES FOR ORTHOGRAPHIC PROJECTIONS

»   Do not randomly place principal views and mix their locations on a drawing.

»   Views must have proper alignment and orientation.

»   It is not necessary to have all six views to describe an object.

»   Simple objects can be illustrated using only two views. Complex objects may need additional views to fully display their information.

»   Scaling must be the same between principal views.

2.4.1 Examples of correct and incorrect orthographic projections

Example 1: Incorrect scaling and poor view alignment:

» All principal views must have the same scale.

» All views must be lined up.
  • In the following example, the bottom view must be directly below the front view.
  • The top view must be directly above the front view.
  • Front, side, and back views must be aligned.

EXAMPLE 1: Incorrect scaling and poor view alignment

Example 2: Incorrect view arrangement:

» Top view must be located above the front view.

» Side views must be located next to the front view.

EXAMPLE 2: Incorrect view arrangement

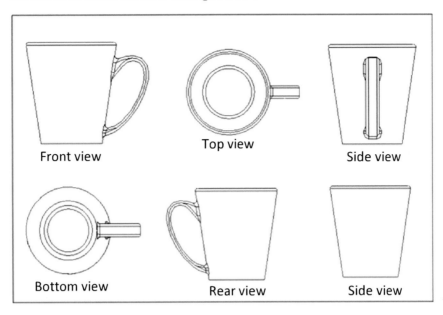

Front view   Top view   Side view

Bottom view   Rear view   Side view

Example 3: Proper scaling and view arrangement:

» Three principal views and the section view have the same scale and are aligned.

» The view arrangement is accurate.

» These views have enough information to describe the detail of the cup. Section views will be discussed in Chapter 4.

EXAMPLE 3: Proper scaling and view alignment

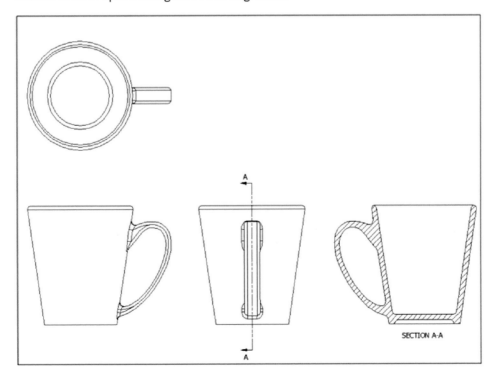

SECTION A-A

Exercise 2.1. Sketch three orthographic views from the following pictorial drawing.

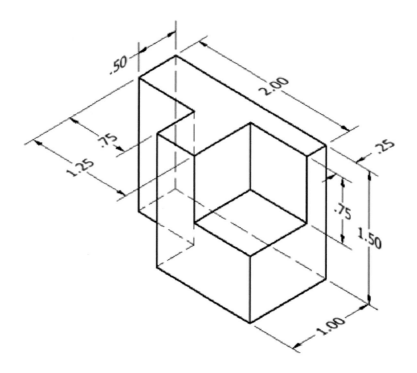

Exercise 2.2. Sketch three orthographic views from the following pictorial drawing.

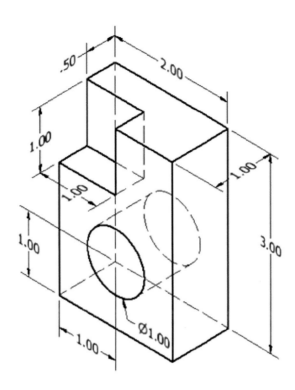

Exercise 2.3. Sketch three orthographic views from the following pictorial drawing.

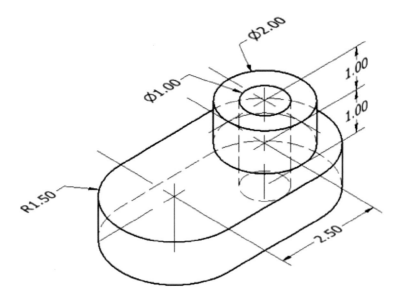

Exercise 2.4. Sketch three orthographic views from the following pictorial drawing.

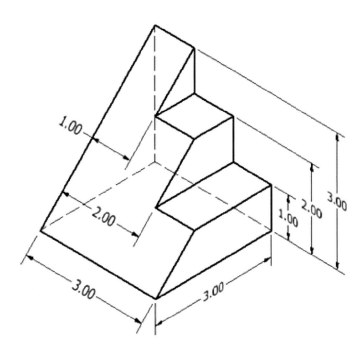

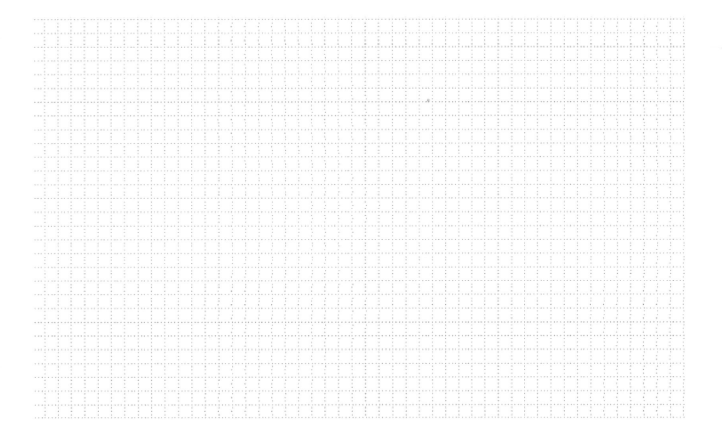

Exercise 2.5. Sketch three orthographic views from the following pictorial drawing.

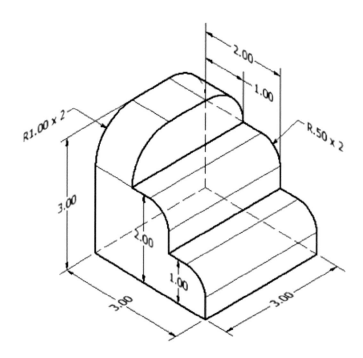

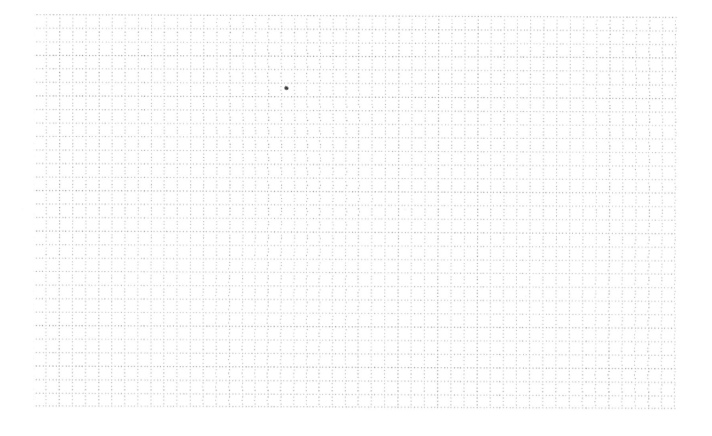

Exercise 2.6. Sketch three orthographic views from the following pictorial drawing.

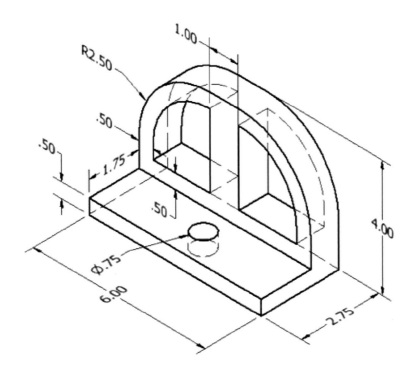

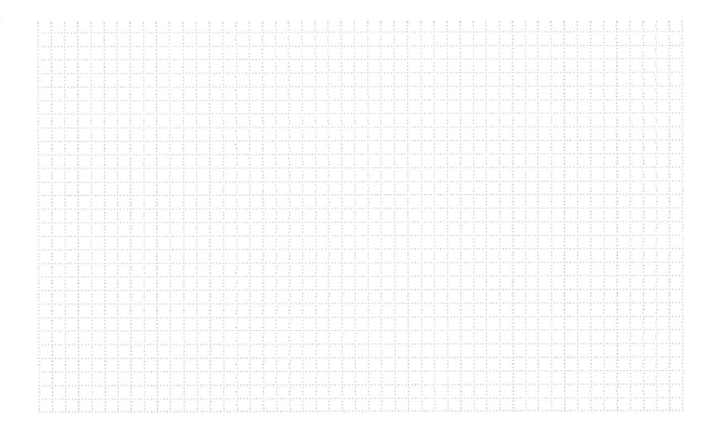

Exercise 2.7. Sketch three orthographic views from the following pictorial drawing.

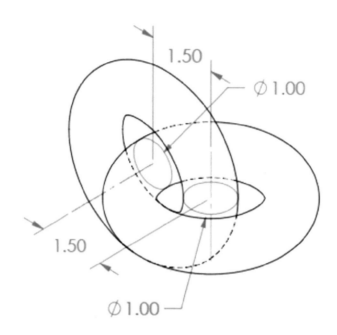

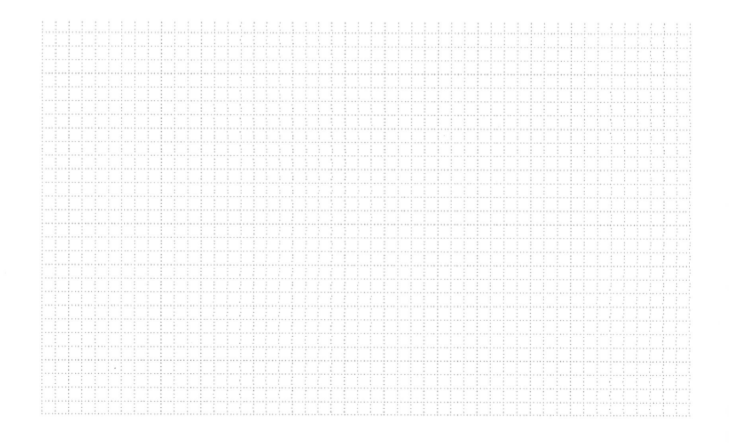

Exercise 2.8. Sketch three orthographic views from the following pictorial drawing.

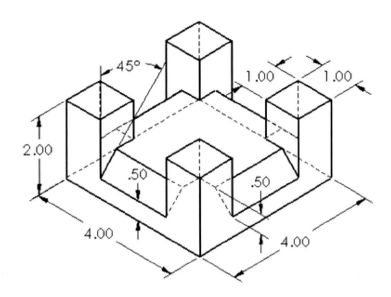

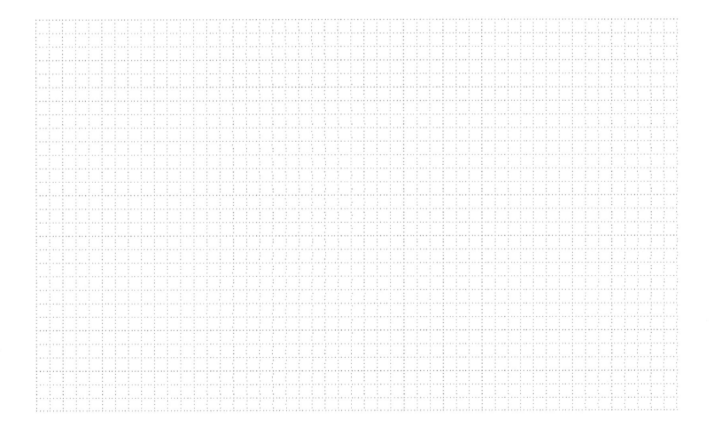

Exercise 2.9. Sketch three orthographic views from the following pictorial drawing.

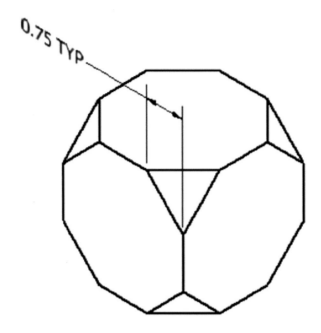

Exercise 2.10. Sketch three orthographic views from the following pictorial drawing.

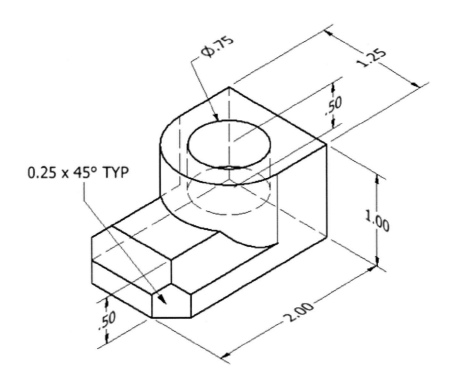

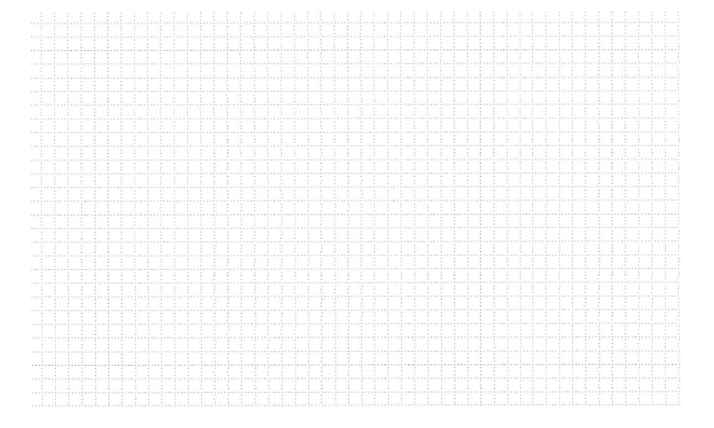

Exercise 2.11. Draw a top view from the following front and side views.

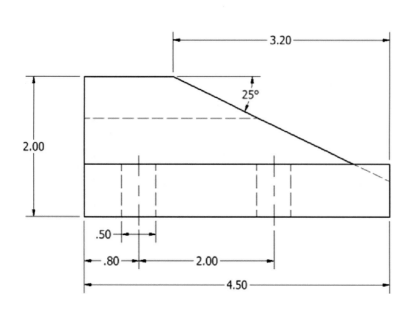

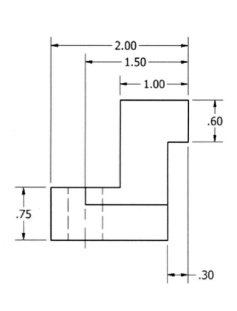

Exercise 2.12. Draw a top view from the following front and side views.

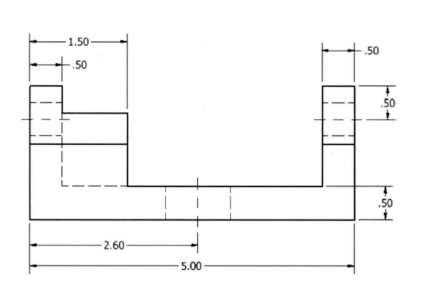

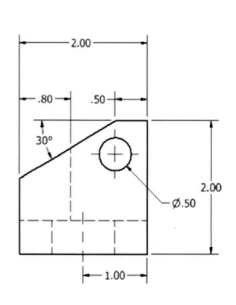

DIMENSIONING AND TOLERANCING

Dimensions are essential element of technical drawings since orthographic projections only describes the shape of an object. A detailed drawing requires size descriptions on necessary orthographic views and specifications, such as materials, finish and tolerance…etc., to fully describe the object and its features. More importantly, when designing parts and assemblies, it is necessary to dimension each component accurately because the dimensions of one may affect other components and the general design of the main assembly. Any dimensioning error in the drawing can cause unaffordable financial damage. In many cases, dimensions and required tolerance of the parts can play an important role in choosing appropriate manufacturing processes which requires extensive experience and knowledge in the field.

In general, there are several dimensioning standards available around the world. In this book, the examples and exercises are based primarily on ANSI (American National Standard Institute) standards which are the common engineering standards in the United States. Other standards used in different countries include:

BSI - British Standards Institute

DIN - Deutsches Institut für Normung

GB - Guojia Biaozhun Standards

ISO - International Standardization Organization

JIS - Japanese Industrial Standards

3.1 TYPES OF DIMENSIONS AND TECHNIQUES

» A *Linear dimension* consists of a dimension value, dimension arrows, dimension lines, and extension lines as shown in Figure 3.1. This type of dimension can be applied horizontally, vertically, and as aligned. Figure 3.2 shows examples of horizontal and vertical linear dimensions with different application techniques demonstrating how the dimension value is located when space is limited. In addition, the figure also demonstrates how the aligned dimension is employed.

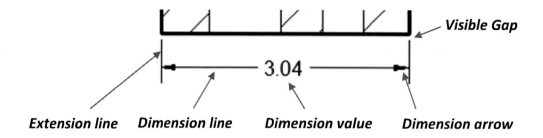

FIGURE 3.1: A linear dimension and its components

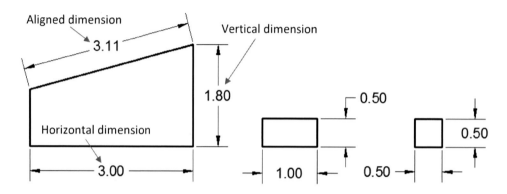

FIGURE 3.2: Examples of horizontal, vertical, and aligned dimensions

» An *Angular dimension* is similar to a linear dimension. It consists of dimension arrows, dimension lines, dimension value, and extension lines as shown in Figure 3.3. However, it requires extension lines only on an as needed basis. Figure 3.4 shows examples of angular dimensions with different application techniques demonstrating how the extension lines are used and how the dimension value is located when space is limited.

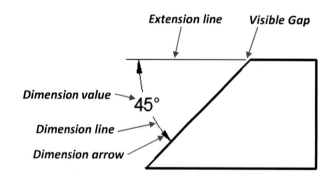

FIGURE 3.3: An angular dimension and its components

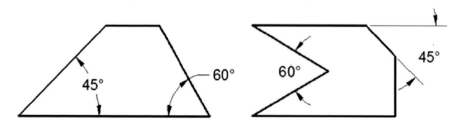

FIGURE 3.4: Examples of angular dimensions

»   *Radial/Diametrical dimensions* consist of a leader line, a dimension arrow, a dimension symbol and value as shown in Figure 3.5. In particular, the symbol "R" is used when the dimension indicates a radius of an arc. The symbol "Ø" is used when the dimension indicates a diameter of a circle. In both cases, the arrow should start from or point to the center. Figure 3.6 shows examples of radial and diametrical dimensions with different application techniques.

Note: It is a common practice to dimension an arc with a radial dimension and a circle with a diametrical dimension.

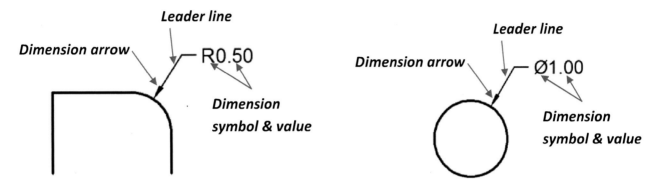

FIGURE 3.5: Radial/Diametrical dimensions and their components

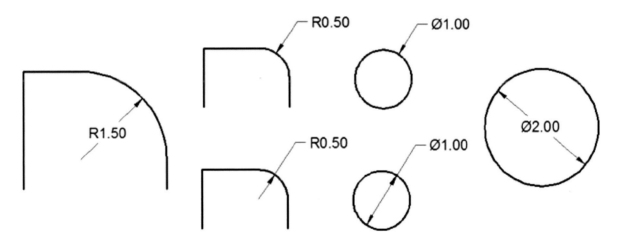

FIGURE 3.6: Examples of Radial/Diametrical dimensions

»   An *ordinate dimension* indicates the horizontal or vertical distance from an origin point. It consists of a dimension line and a dimension value. This type of dimensioning technique is widely used in the electronic industry where engineers have to specify many holes on circuit boards for the drilling process. Figure 3.7 shows an example of ordinate dimensions indicating center points of the circles.

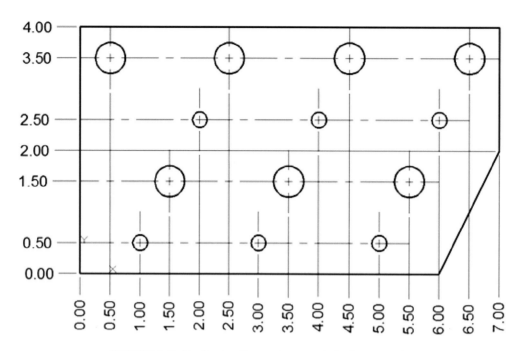

FIGURE 3.7: Ordinate dimensions and their examples

3.2 DIMENSIONING SPECIFICATIONS

As discussed in Chapter 1, the size of dimensions can vary depending on the scale of the drawing. However, the scale should remain consistent throughout the drawing. It is also recommended to follow the general dimension specification as shown in Figure 3.8.

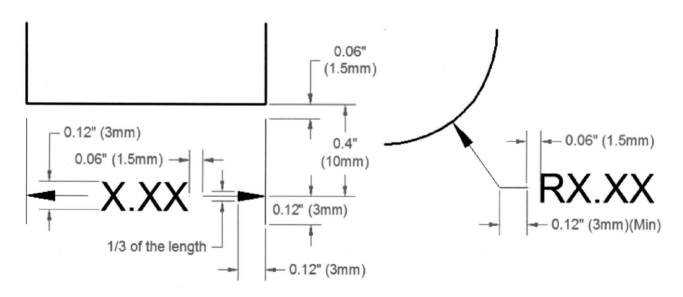

FIGURE 3.8: Recommended dimensioning specification

3.3 RULES AND PRACTICES

There are some general rules and practices that we must follow in order to create an appropriate technical drawing:

» Dimension lines and extension lines should be thinner than the visible lines of the object to avoid confusion in the drawing.

» Dimension lines and extension lines must be solid lines (i.e. do not use hidden lines).

» If possible, avoid crossing dimension lines and extension lines. Place shorter dimensions before longer ones.

» Centerlines may be used as extension lines when necessary.

» Use centerlines to indicate round features (e.g. holes, shafts, and cylinders ... etc.) and the symmetry of the object.

» Centerlines must extend beyond round features or symmetry objects.

» Dimension text should have the minimum height of 0.12" (3mm) and should be uniform throughout the drawing.

» Do not place dimension text on any lines or objects.

» Do not place dimensions on hidden lines. Create sectional views and place dimensions on them instead.

» Place dimension text in the horizontal direction.

» Place dimension text midway between the arrowheads whenever possible.

» There should be a visible gap between an extension line and the object.

» If possible, avoid placing dimensions inside the object.

» Dimensions should not be too close to the object or too far away from the object. In general, dimensions should be at least 0.4" (10mm) away from the object and subsequent dimensions should be at least 0.25" (6mm) away from each other.

» If the dimensions are too crowded, scale up the view to gain extra space or use detailed views.

» Use a radial dimension to dimension an arc and a diametrical dimension to dimension a circle.

3.4 TOLERANCING

In reality, it is extremely difficult for manufacturers to mass produce a product that is identical to its nominal dimensions. Material thermal expansion, machine vibration, wear and tear on tooling, and many other factors can easily cause dimension deviation during manufacturing. Allowing certain tolerances on dimensions can ease manufacturing processes, reduce rejects, and increase production rate. When a product is to be manufactured, engineers must assign proper tolerance on each dimension of the product. Manufacturers will then target the nominal dimensions with maximum acceptable deviation to maintain product quality. Depending on the design requirement, products can have as little as one standard tolerance on all dimensions or many different tolerances on them.

Engineers determine tolerances based on product applications. Unreasonably applying tight tolerances on a part will not benefit the design. It will only increase difficulty in manufacturing. If a product (e.g. pencil holder, coffee mug, and flower pot) does not require tight tolerance in size, enforcing tight tolerance all over the design will only increase the price of the product and lower the market competitiveness. On the other hand, if the design involved an assembly with multiple components, it is recommended to apply tight tolerance in some areas to assure the components can be joined together and maintain product quality.

3.4.1 Types of fit

In order to determine tolerances for different design applications, it is necessary to understand types of fit. Table 3.1 shows the general idea of clearance fit, transition fit, and interference fit.

TABLE 3.1 Types of fit

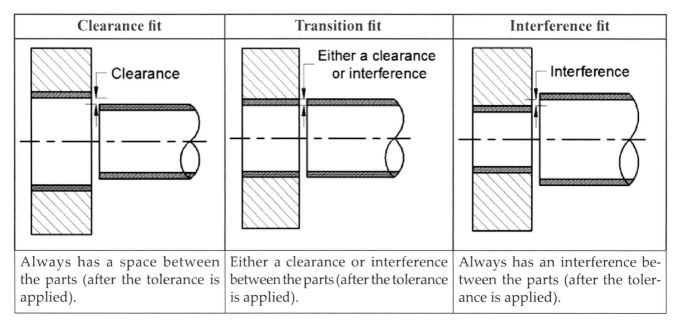

Clearance fit	Transition fit	Interference fit
Always has a space between the parts (after the tolerance is applied).	Either a clearance or interference between the parts (after the tolerance is applied).	Always has an interference between the parts (after the tolerance is applied).

3.4.2 Types of tolerance

The commonly used methods to specify tolerances in dimensions include Unilateral, Bilateral, Limits, and Block tolerances. Below are some examples and explanations for these tolerances.

» **Unilateral**

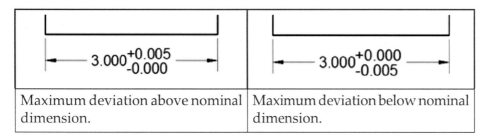

Maximum deviation above nominal dimension.	Maximum deviation below nominal dimension.

» **Bilateral**

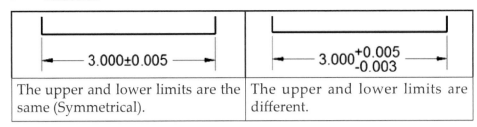

The upper and lower limits are the same (Symmetrical).	The upper and lower limits are different.

» **Limits**

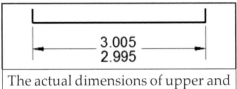

The actual dimensions of upper and lower limits are specified.

» **Block tolerance**

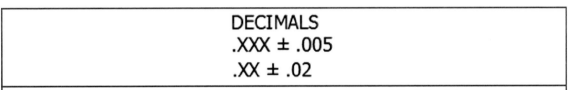

A general note that applies to all dimensions that are not specified. In this example, when a dimension shows three digits after the decimal point, the tolerance of that dimension is ±0.005. Similarly, a dimension shows two digits after the decimal point, the tolerance of that dimension is ±0.02.

In this book, we briefly introduce **Types of fit** and **Types of tolerance.** Please refer to engineering handbooks for details on types of fit and Geometric Dimensioning and Tolerancing (GD&T) handbooks for additional methods in specifying tolerance.

3.4.3 Tolerance Accumulation

Although knowing the type of tolerance and fit can determine proper tolerances for a product, dimension arrangement is also an important factor that can affect the tolerance of the product. For example, linear dimensions can be chained continuously or can be applied from the same datum depending on the design specification of the object as shown in Figure 3.9. The dimensioning technique is important because it can negatively affect the manufacturing process and critical dimensions of the object. The examples in Figure 3.9 shows that dimensions applied from the same datum can prevent accumulative errors. The figure indicates that each dimension allows 0.01" deviation, the total height tolerance of the example on the left can be as much as 0.03" while the right one is only 0.01".

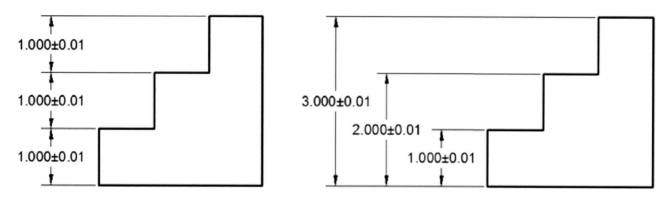

FIGURE 3.9: Tolerance accumulation: Linear dimensions chained continuously (Left), Linear dimensions applied from the same datum (Right)

ADDITIONAL VIEWS

When the six principal views cannot effectively describe complex objects, additional views such as, **section views**, **detail views**, **broken views**, and **auxiliary views** are necessary to support the principal views and better describe the objects.

4.1 SECTIONAL VIEWS

Although hidden lines can describe hidden features within an object, visualizing these lines can be confusing and difficult to readers. The use of sectional views, however, will provide a clear description of hidden features within orthographic projections. The concept of sectional views is to create an imaginary cutting plane across the object and visualize this cross-sectional area as shown in Figure 4.1. The sectional view is an extension of projected views and should be labeled as "SECTION X-X", where X-X are capital letters starting from A to Z. In this book, several types of sectional views will be discussed.

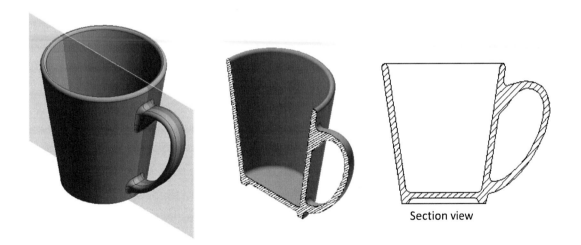

Section view

FIGURE 4.1: Concept of sectional view

4.1.1 Construction of sectional views

» Choose a base view to show where the imaginary cutting plane is.

» Use a cutting plane line to identify the cutting plane.

» Assign the viewing direction.

» Place the new sectional view next to the projected view (apply the orthographic projection rule).

» Label the sectional view using SECTION A-A, B-B, or C-C and so on.

» Apply section lines ONLY to the cross-sectional area.

» Show remaining visible area.

» Avoid using hidden lines in sectional views.

4.1.2 Line types used in sectional views

» Cutting plane lines

The purpose of cutting plane lines is to show where the imaginary cutting plane is and indicate the viewing direction. These lines take precedence over centerlines. Figure 4.2 shows the general specification of cutting plane lines.

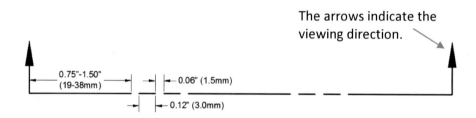

The arrows indicate the viewing direction.

0.75"-1.50" (19-38mm)   0.06" (1.5mm)

0.12" (3.0mm)

FIGURE 4.2: Cutting plane line specification

» Section lines

The purpose of section lines is to indicate the cross-sectional areas where the imaginary cutting plane has cut through. Section lines are typically a set of thin lines at 45° or 135° that are parallel to each other as shown in Figure 4.3. Other angles such as 30° or 60° can also be used when necessary. Attention should be paid to avoid drawing section lines parallel to visible lines.

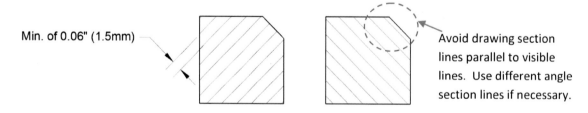

Min. of 0.06" (1.5mm)

Avoid drawing section lines parallel to visible lines. Use different angle section lines if necessary.

FIGURE 4.3: Section line specifications

4.1.3 Types of sectional views

» Full section

For full sectional view applications, the imaginary cutting plane (a flat plane) is visualized to pass through the entire object. Figure 4.4 demonstrates that full sectional views can be applied into different areas to visually reveal the hidden features within the same object. Using the rule of Third angle projection, the sectional views are created from the base view and are placed opposite to the arrows of the cutting plane lines. The figure also illustrates that visible lines must be shown within the section views though they are not part of the cross-sectional area.

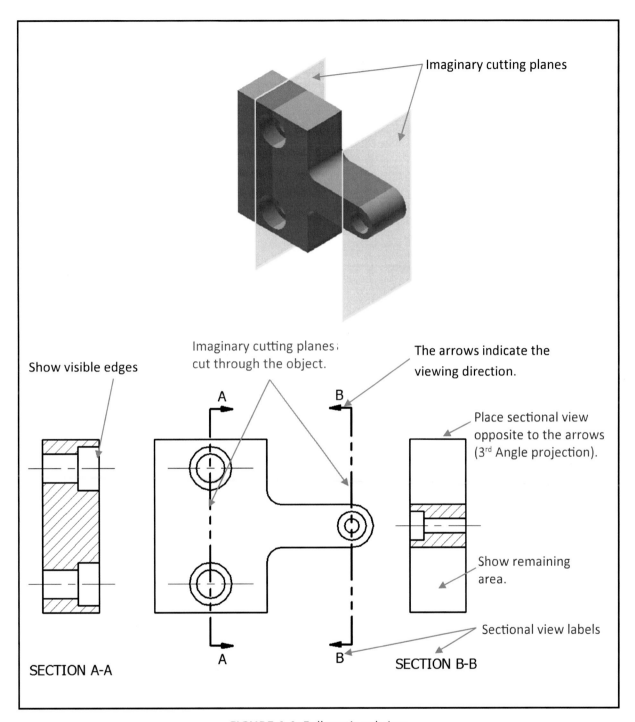

Imaginary cutting planes

Imaginary cutting planes cut through the object.

The arrows indicate the viewing direction.

Show visible edges

Place sectional view opposite to the arrows (3rd Angle projection).

Show remaining area.

Sectional view labels

SECTION A-A

SECTION B-B

FIGURE 4.4: Full sectional view

» Half section

Unlike full sectional views, the imaginary cutting plane used in this kind of views has a 90° bend and passes through a portion of the object. Only portions of the projected view are sectioned and the remaining area remains the same. Half sectional is mainly used for cylindrical or symmetrical objects (Figure 4.5).

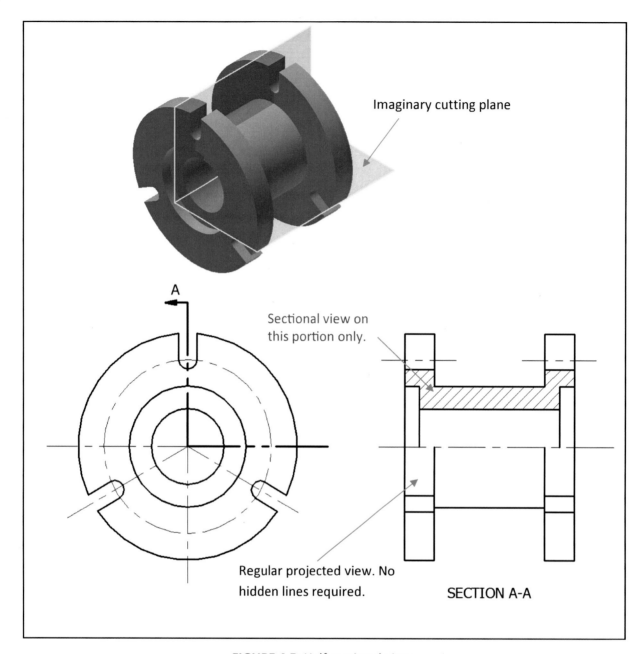

FIGURE 4.5: Half sectional view

»   Offset section

Offset sectional views allow users to display several hidden features in different locations in one sectional view instead of multiple full sectional views. The imaginary cutting plane can have several 90° bends passing through different features of an object as demonstrated in Figure 4.6. All bends on the cutting plane are required to be 90°.

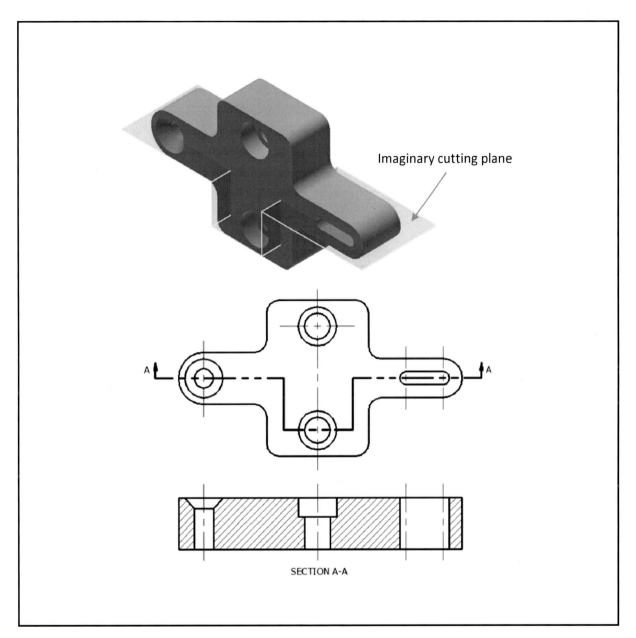

FIGURE 4.6: Offset sectional view

» Aligned section

The imaginary cutting plane for this application can be bent at the center of the object. Its function is to show features within the object at a certain angle as demonstrated in Figure 4.7.

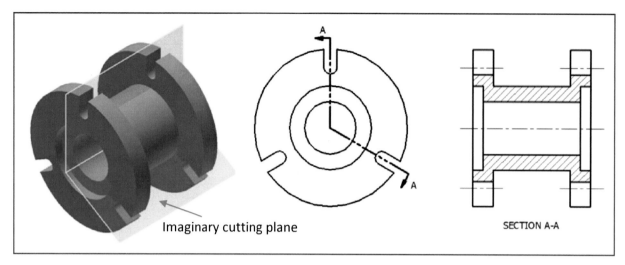

FIGURE 4.7: Aligned sectional view

> » Broken-out section

In some applications, a full sectional view may be too large for a small feature. It is recommended to use a broken-out section within a projected view as demonstrated in Figure 4.8.

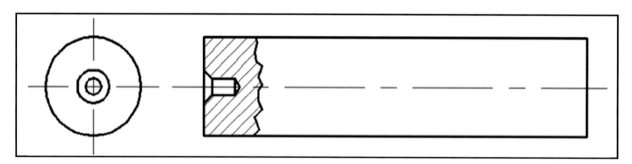

FIGURE 4.8: Broken-out sectional view

4.2 DETAIL VIEWS

A detail view is an extended view from a projected view. The view is used to enlarge details of an area where it may be too crowded for dimensioning. The view should be scaled up to gain extra spacing but dimensions must remain unchanged. The scaling factor depends on the details of the object. Figure 4.9 shows an example of a detail view.

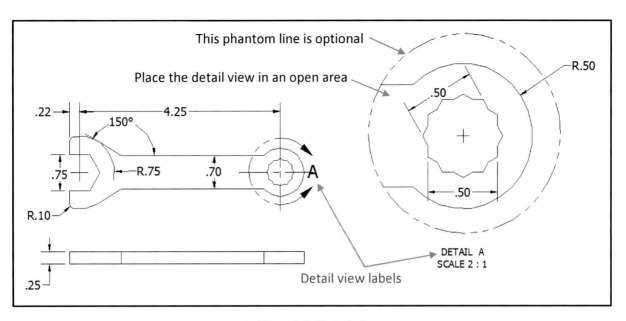

FIGURE 4.9: Detail view

4.3 BROKEN VIEWS

A broken view is not an extension of any projected views. It is a great method to display long objects with a constant cross-sectional area. Small features within a long object are usually unnoticeable when displayed together with the long object in full scale. Hiding the repeated long section virtually allows proper dimensioning for small features as illustrated in Figure 4.10.

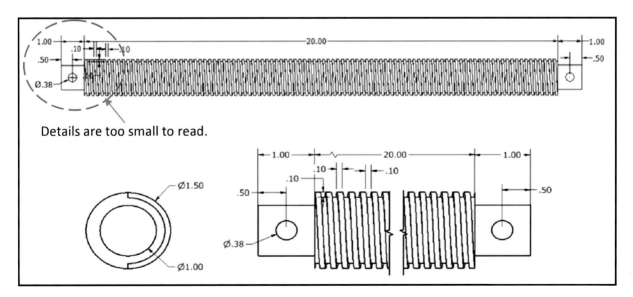

FIGURE 4.10: Broken view

4.4 AUXILIARY VIEWS

The purpose of auxiliary views is to display important features on an inclined surface with true dimensions. Unlike the six principal views, an auxiliary view is projected and placed parallel to the inclined surface where it cannot be illustrated clearly by the principal views. Figure 4.11 shows an example of an auxiliary view.

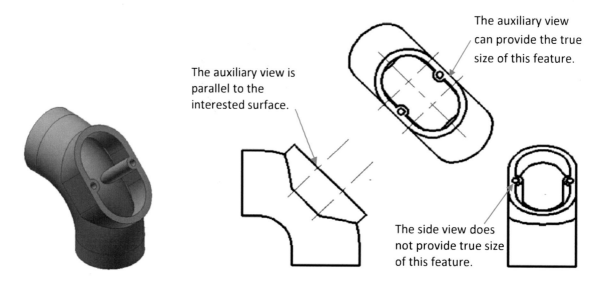

FIGURE 4.11: Auxiliary view

Exercises- Chapter 4

Draw two principal views and a sectional view for the following exercises.

Exercise 4.1

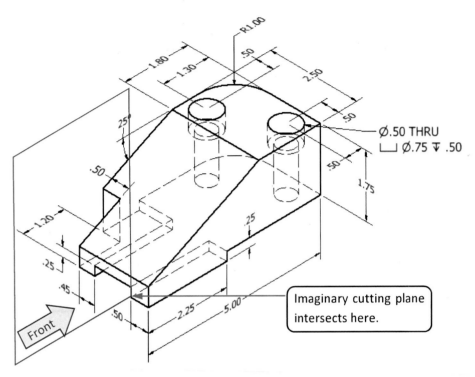

R1.00
1.80
1.30
.50
2.50
.50
25°
Ø.50 THRU
⌴ Ø.75 ⊽ .50
.50
.50
1.75
.50
.25
1.20
.25
.25
.95
2.25
5.00
.50

Front

Imaginary cutting plane intersects here.

Exercise 4.2

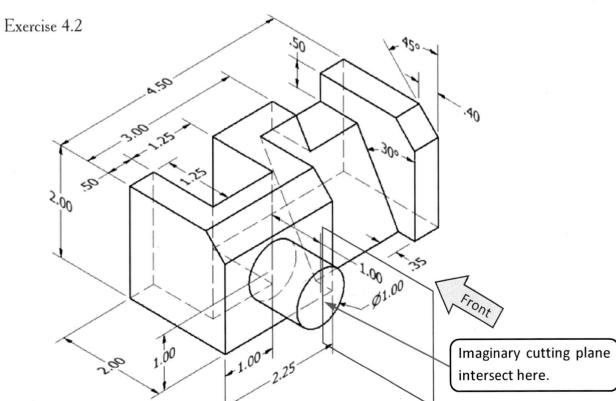

.50
45°
4.50
.40
3.00
1.25
30°
.50
1.25
2.00
1.00
.35
1.00
Ø1.00
Front
2.00
1.00
1.00
2.25

Imaginary cutting plane intersect here.

Draw two principal views and a sectional view for the following exercises.

Exercise 4.3

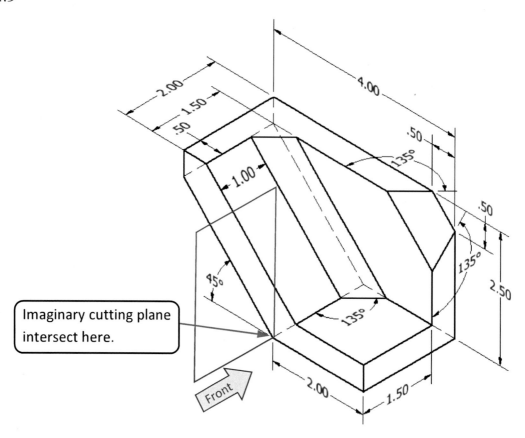

Imaginary cutting plane intersect here.

Exercise 4.4

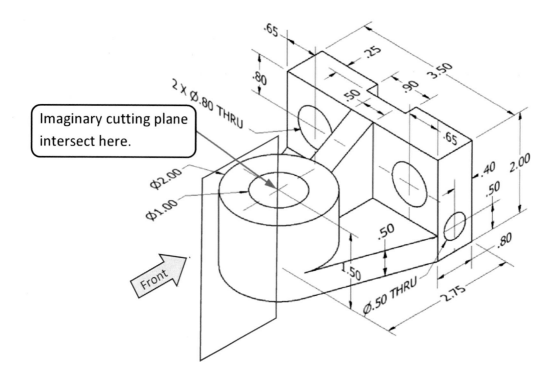

Imaginary cutting plane intersect here.

Exercise 4.5. Draw a sectional view from the following front and side views.

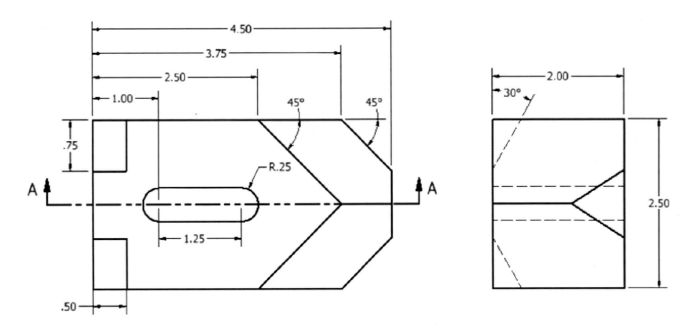

Exercise 4.6. Draw a sectional view from the following front and side views.

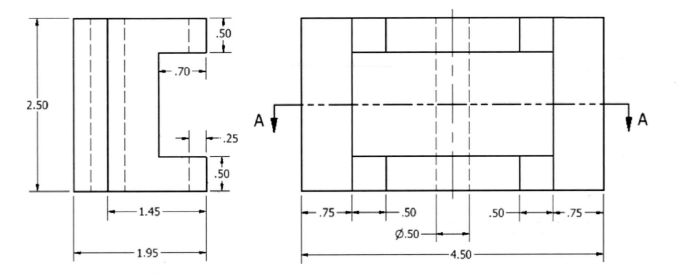

PICTORIAL SKETCHING (ISOMETRIC VIEW)

Orthographic drawings are very useful to present and communicate design ideas between individuals. However, understanding orthographic projection can be difficult for beginners in designs and engineering as it requires necessary training for interpretation. Pictorial drawings, on the other hand, are easy to read and requires no skill from readers. They are make-believe 3D drawings and are one of the best ways to present conceptual ideas.

There are three types of pictorial drawings, namely, **Axonometric** (which includes isometric, diametric, and trimetric), **Oblique**, and **Perspective**. Among these drawing types, isometric is one of the most commonly used pictorial drawings in many engineering applications as demonstrated in examples throughout this book. In this chapter, we will only cover the construction method of isometric drawings.

5.1 BASIC CONCEPT OF ISOMETRIC DRAWINGS

The three principal axes (X,Y,Z) in isometric drawings are separated 60° apart, in which two of them are 30° from a horizontal line, and one of them is perpendicular to the horizontal line as shown in Figure 5.1.

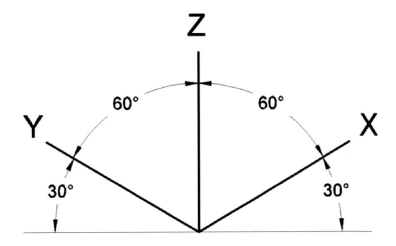

FIGURE 5.1: Three principal axes in isometric drawings

Straight lines and arcs are the main elements in isometric drawings. For straight edges that are parallel to the principal axes, the lines are drawn in full scale along its direction. For arcs, a special technique will be needed to create the arcs and ellipses. Let us use the following examples to demonstrate how an isometric drawing is constructed using straight lines and arcs.

Example 5.1

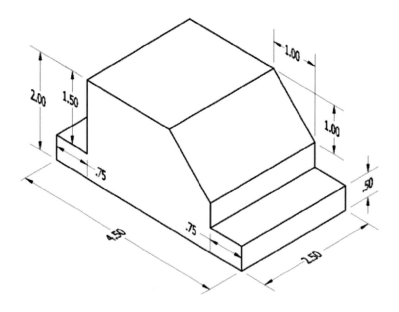

Steps

1	Draw three thin construction lines on the isometric axes (X,Y,Z).

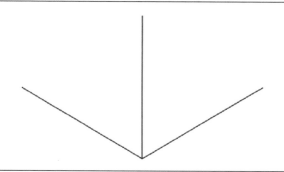

2	Draw three edges of the object in full scale on each principal axis.

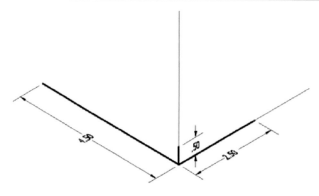

3 Use all the given dimensions and draw all other edges on Y-Z plane.

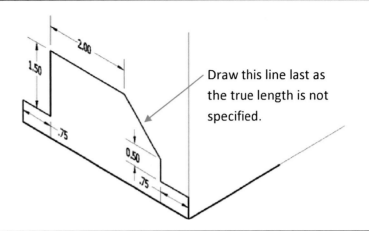

Draw this line last as the true length is not specified.

4 Draw additional thin construction lines using overall size of the object (Draw a box).

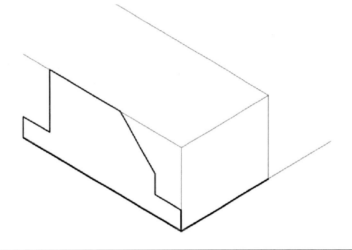

5 Draw all other edges on the other plane that is parallel to the Y-Z plane.

(Use construction lines to help identifying locations).

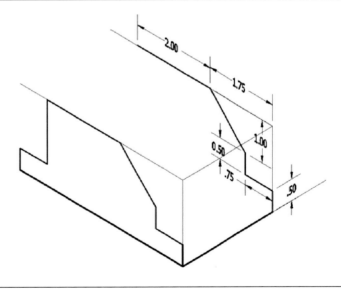

6   Connect end points between two parallel planes. (The lines must be parallel to the principal X axis.)

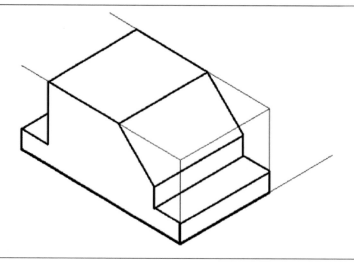

7   Remove the construction lines.

Example 5.2

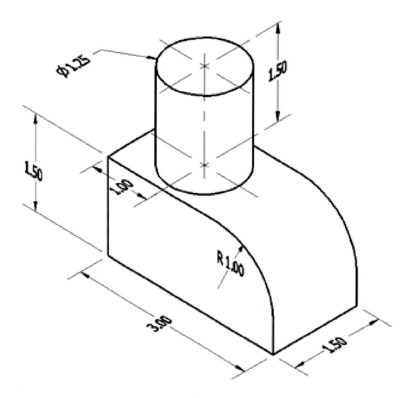

Steps

1. Draw three thin construction lines on the isometric axes (X,Y,Z).

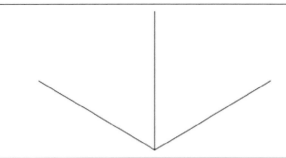

2. Use the given dimensions and draw all straight edges on Y-Z and X-Z planes.

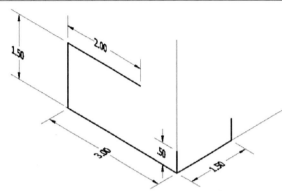

3. Draw construction boxes using thin lines for the base and the cylinder separately, include the centerlines for the cylinder.

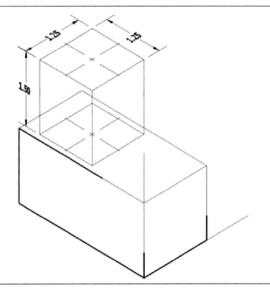

4. Draw 4 additional construction lines on the top of the construction box as shown.

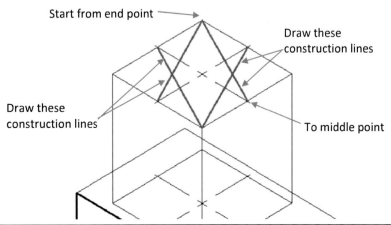

Start from end point

Draw these construction lines

Draw these construction lines

To middle point

5   Draw two arcs using the newly defined centers and radii (R).

Note: the length of a R is the distance between the center point and the outer edge of the construction box.

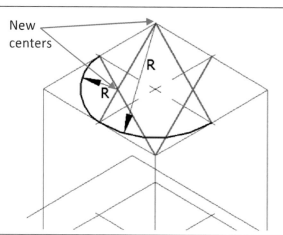

6   Repeat Step 5 for the arc on the top and on the right.

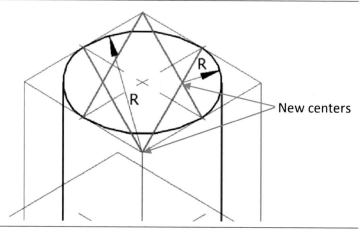

7   Repeat steps 4 and 6 to draw the bottom of the cylinder (But draw only half of the ellipse). Connect the ellipses using straight lines.

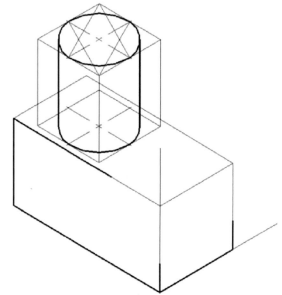

8   Draw new construction lines for the rounded edge (Treat it as a full circle).

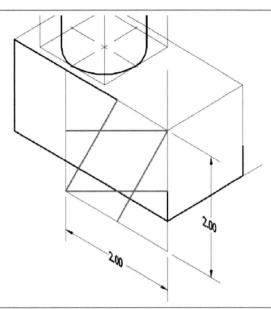

9   Draw an arc using the newly defined center and radius.

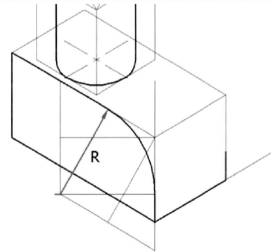

10 Repeat steps 8 and 9 to draw the rounded edge on the other side.

Draw the remaining straight edges.

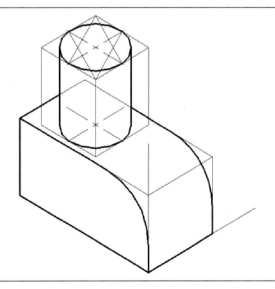

11 Remove the construction lines.

5.2 TANGENT EDGES

In reality, tangent edges are obscured to readers because there are no visible hard edges shown between tangent features. By indicating the tangent edges on the views, particularly in isometric views, it can help readers to clearly specify the seams between features. A tangent edge is a thin continuous line. It is optional to display tangent edges on the drawings. Figure 5.2 shows an example of isometric drawings with and without tangent edges.

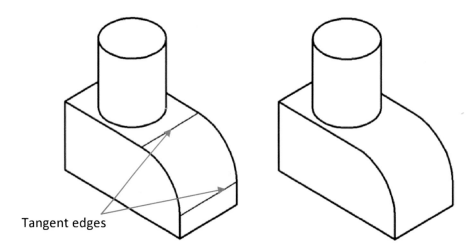

Tangent edges

FIGURE 5.2: Isometric drawings with and without tangent edges

Exercise 5.1 Sketch a pictorial drawing from the following drawing.

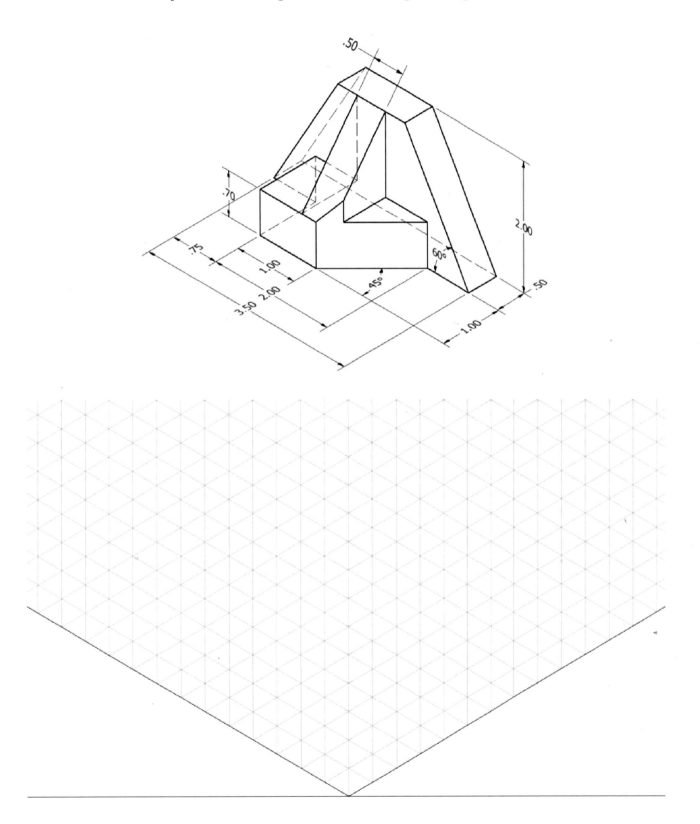

Exercise 5.2 Sketch a pictorial drawing from the following drawing.

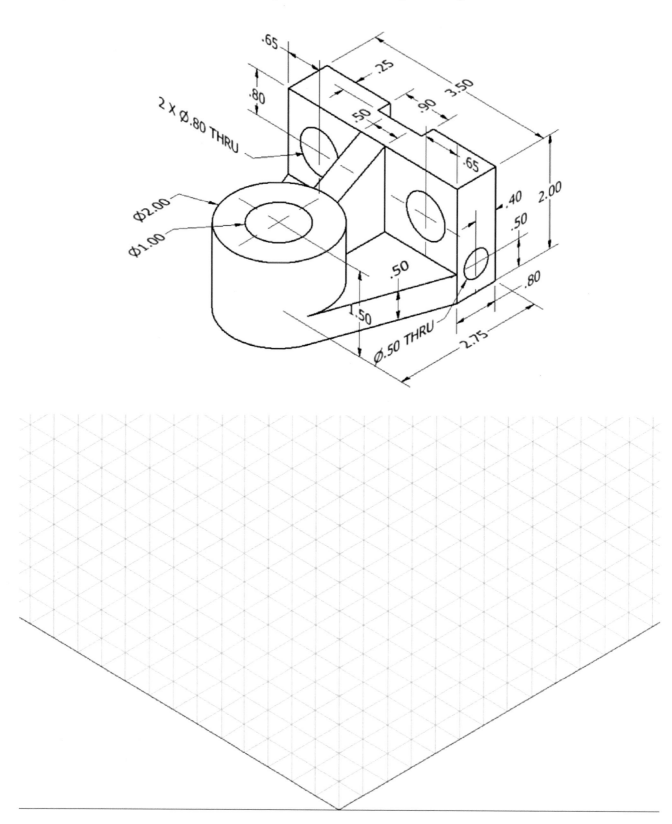

INTRODUCTION TO AUTOCAD (ACAD)

AutoCAD, a computer aided design (CAD) software program, has been widely used by architects and civil, mechanical, and manufacturing engineers for more than two decades. Companies prefer this CAD program as their main drafting tool for their products because it increases the productivity of the engineers and has many advantages over manual drafting. The following are some highlights of AutoCAD:

» Unlimited drawing space (Users do not need to predefine paper size).

» Drawings can be edited quickly without damaging the originals.

» Drawings can be reproduced without losing their clarity.

» Drawings can be scaled in both directions without sacrificing their clarity.

» Drawings are highly accurate.

This chapter introduces the environment, methods of commanding, and the basics of AutoCAD 2015.

6.1 WORKSPACES

Three standard workspaces are available in AutoCAD to better accommodate different drawing tasks. They are interchangeable and namely, **Drafting & Annotation**, **3D Basics**, and **3D Modeling**. For the purpose of this book, we focus mainly on the **Drafting & Annotation** workspace which can be selected from the following options as shown in Figure 6.1.

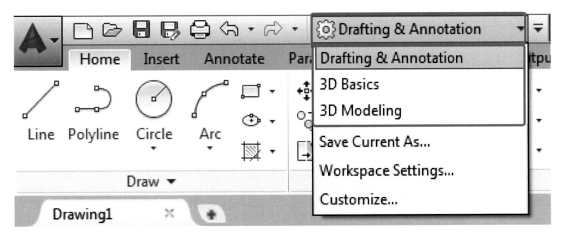

FIGURE 6.1: Choice of workspaces in AutoCAD

6.2 USER INTERFACE

The user interface of AutoCAD contains a **Graphics Window**, a **Status Bar**, a **Quick Access Toolbar**, a **Ribbon (Tabs and Panels)**, and a **Command Line Window**. Figure 6.2 shows an example of the AutoCAD environment. In order to operate the software program efficiently, users must pay high attention to the **Command Line Window** as it will show any error of command applications and display necessary steps for each command.

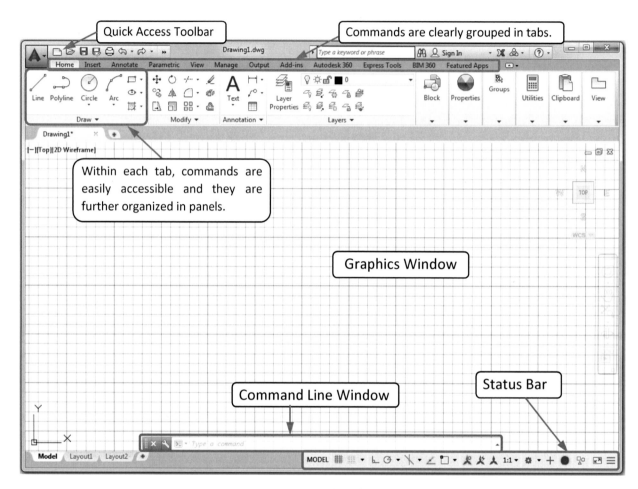

FIGURE 6.2: AutoCAD user interface (Drafting & Annotation)

6.3 METHODS OF COMMANDING

Commands can be entered using the icons on the **Ribbon/toolbars.** They can also be entered directly in the **Command Line Window** or within the **Graphics Window**. At any time, pressing the "**Esc**" key on the keyboard can cancel the command.

6.3.1 Ribbon

Commands can be accessed within the Ribbon. They are grouped and arranged in tabs and panels. Partially or fully minimizing the Ribbon helps expand the viewing space. By clicking on the "Minimize" button on the right side of the tabs, the Ribbon can be toggled into four different layouts as shown in Figure 6.3.

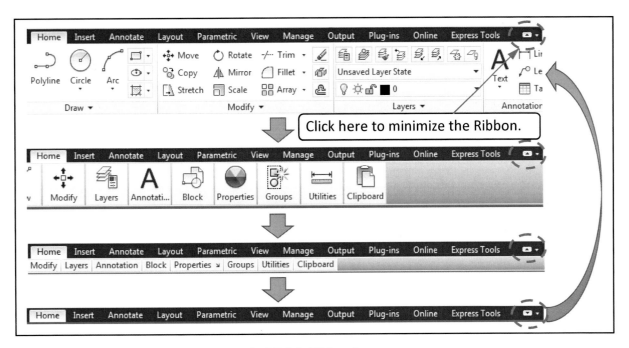

FIGURE 6.3: Ribbon layouts

6.3.2 Command Line Window

This method requires memorization of the commands and their shortcuts. Commands are typed into the Command Line Window. They are relatively easy to remember as they are English words such as LINE, CIRCLE, COPY, and MOVE…etc., and they are not case sensitive. Any typing mistake can be cleared by pressing the "**Esc**" key or corrected by pressing the "**Backspace**" on the keyboard. Most of the exercises in this book use this method of input to demonstrate geometry constructions. The Command Line Window can be closed by clicking on "**X**" on the window as shown in Figure 6.4 or by pressing "**CTRL**" + "**9**" on the keyboard. The window can be reopened by pressing "**CTRL**" + "**9**" again.

FIGURE 6.4: Command Line Window

6.3.3 Graphics Window

Similar to the Command Line Window, commands can be entered anywhere within the Graphics Window when the dynamic input mode is on. Figure 6.5 shows the command example next to the cursor as it was typed. Additional functions of Dynamic input will be discussed later in this chapter (see Relative coordinates).

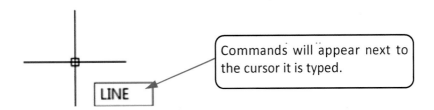

FIGURE 6.5: An example of a command in Graphics Window

6.4 CONTROLLING AND VIEWING

The typical controlling and viewing tools are **ViewCube, Navigation bar,** and **Mouse Wheel**. The **ViewCube** provides users an easy access to manipulate and to view 3D objects in different orientations conveniently. For 2D applications, the **Navigation bar** allows users to zoom in/out of the drawing and to display different areas of the drawing. The **Mouse Wheel** on the mouse provides real time zooming and real time panning without inputting the commands. The detailed explanation for these three viewing tools are as follows.

» ViewCube

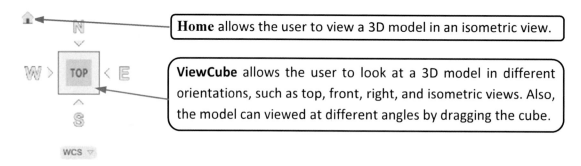

Home allows the user to view a 3D model in an isometric view.

ViewCube allows the user to look at a 3D model in different orientations, such as top, front, right, and isometric views. Also, the model can viewed at different angles by dragging the cube.

» Mouse

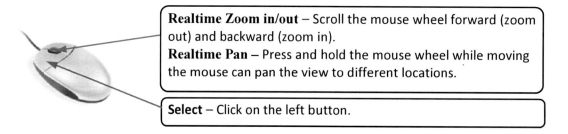

Realtime Zoom in/out – Scroll the mouse wheel forward (zoom out) and backward (zoom in).
Realtime Pan – Press and hold the mouse wheel while moving the mouse can pan the view to different locations.

Select – Click on the left button.

» Navigation bar

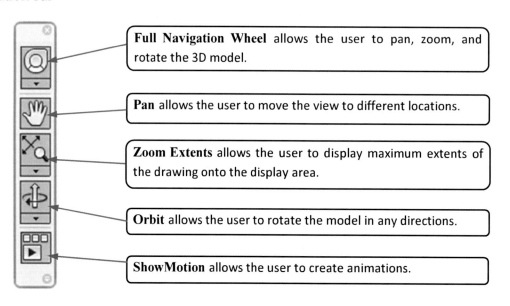

Full Navigation Wheel allows the user to pan, zoom, and rotate the 3D model.

Pan allows the user to move the view to different locations.

Zoom Extents allows the user to display maximum extents of the drawing onto the display area.

Orbit allows the user to rotate the model in any directions.

ShowMotion allows the user to create animations.

6.5 AUTOCAD BASICS

AutoCAD uses Cartesian and polar coordinate systems to create points, lines, and other entities. Before introducing the commands in AutoCAD, it is important to understand the **sign and angle conventions** of the program and the **absolute and relative coordinate systems** used in the program.

6.5.1 Sign conventions

Positive X is located to right of the origin.

Negative X is located to left of the origin

Positive Y is located above the origin.

Negative Y is located below the origin.

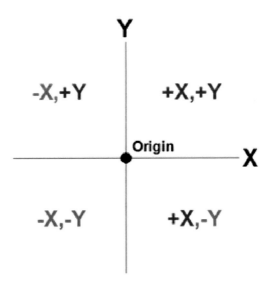

6.5.2 Angle convention

All angle measurements are counterclockwise and starts from the east (0°).

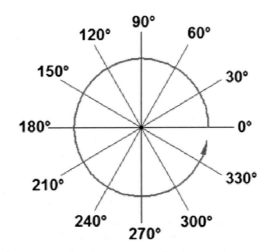

6.5.3 Absolute and relative coordinate systems

In AutoCAD, lines can be created by entering the coordinates of two points as shown in Figure 6.6. For example, in absolute Cartesian coordinates, the figure indicates that the XY coordinates of the first and second points are (2,3) and (4,6) respectively. However, in relative coordinates, the XY coordinates of the second point is (2,3) because it considers the previous point as (0,0).

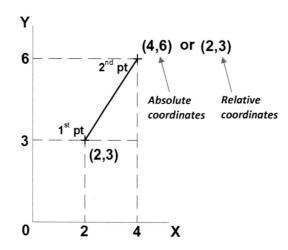

FIGURE 6.6: Absolute vs relative coordinates in Cartesian coordinate system

For the polar coordinate system, the points are defined by the distance between two points and the angle from the X axis as shown in Figure 6.7. In absolute polar coordinates, the first point in the figure is 3 units long from the origin and 30 degree from the X-axis. The second point is 5.8 units long from the origin and 45 degrees from the X-axis. However in relative coordinates, the second point is 3 units long from the previous point and 60 degrees from the X-axis. Although using the polar coordinate system may seem complicated, it is a very useful coordinate system in geometry construction when an angle is given.

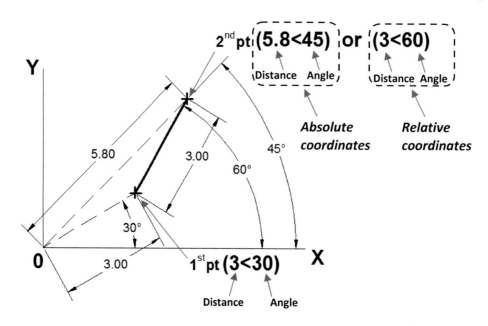

FIGURE 6.7: Absolute vs relative coordinates in polar coordinate system

» Relative coordinates

When starting a new drawing, Dynamic Input  is turned on by system default. If it is off for any reason, turn the Dynamic Input on to activate the relative coordinate mode. Dynamic Input mode can be toggled on and off by pressing the function key "**F12**" on the keyboard or by clicking on its icon on the status bar as shown.

Note: If the Dynamic Input icon is not available on the status bar, use the following steps to add the Dynamic Input icon onto the status bar.

1. Click on the customization icon on the status bar.

2. Check Dynamic input.

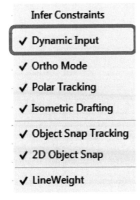

3.

» Absolute coordinates

To activate the absolute coordinate mode, turn the Dynamic Input off. Some advanced users prefer to stay on the absolute mode during the drawing construction process and use the relative mode on an as needed basis by using the symbol "@" in front of the coordinates. For example, @4,6 (Cartesian coordinate system) and @3<30 (Polar coordinate system). The symbol "@" activates the relative coordinate mode temporarily during a coordinate entry.

DRAWING SETUPS AND PLOTTING

Drawing units, scale, drawing limits, and title blocks should be properly defined before starting a drawing because the appropriate drawing environment can reduce the chance of getting errors in the drawing. This chapter introduces several useful setup and plotting procedures for a typical AutoCAD drawing.

7.1 DRAWING UNITS

In AutoCAD, one drawing unit could represent one inch, one foot, one centimeter, or one kilometer. Users can switch between the units; however, the size of the object will not be scaled accordingly. In other words, AutoCAD does not do the conversion automatically. This unit option scales the geometry rather than converting it. For example, when switching the unit from inches to meters for a one inch long line, the one inch long line will become a one meter long line.

7.1.1 How to setup drawing units for drawings

1. Enable the Drawing Units dialog box by entering **UNITS** in the Command Line Window or by the clicking on the application icon, Drawing Utilities, Units as shown.

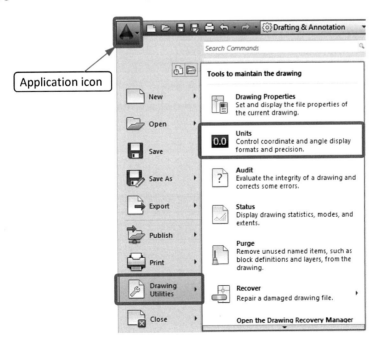

2. For the purpose of this book, use the default settings as shown.

>   Length Types (**Decimal**) and precision (**0.0000**).

>   Angle Types (**Decimal Degrees**) and precision (**0**).

>   Insertion scale (**Inches**).

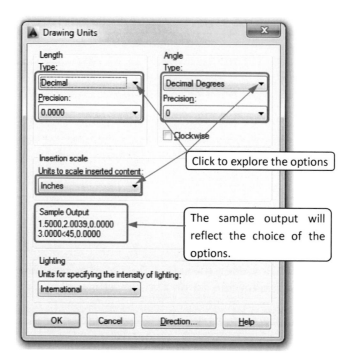

New AutoCAD users should explore the options of each setting and read the **sample output** to get familiar with the output options. Note: These settings are for measurement and coordinate display only; do not confuse them with dimensions.

7.2 DRAWING LIMITS

Drawing limits in AutoCAD sets an invisible drawing boundary in the drawing area which can be used for defining sheet size for the drawing. However, it is not mandatory to set drawing limits for every drawing, particularly for geometry that is larger than a standard drawing sheet.

7.2.1 Functions of drawing limits

>   When drawing limits is turned on, you cannot enter points outside the limits.

>   When drawing limits is turned off, you can enter points inside and outside the limits. This is the default setting.

7.2.2 How to turn drawing limits on or off

>   Enter **LIMITS** in the Command Line Window.

>   Enter **ON** to turn the limits on or **OFF** to turn the limits off.

7.2.3 How to set drawing limits

»   Enter **LIMITS** in the Command Line.

»   Specify lower left corner (Enter coordinates).

»   Specify upper right corner (Enter coordinates).

In this book, lessons are created based on the default drawing limits settings, i.e. Drawing limits is turned **off**, the lower left corner <**0.0000,0.0000**> and the upper right corner <**12.0000,9.0000**>.

7.3 TITLE BLOCK

As explained in Chapter 1, a title block is essential in every engineering drawing. It can be drawn in AutoCAD like a regular geometry using the Draw commands, which will be introduced in the later chapters. It can also be inserted from a default template in the program. Before learning the method of inserting default title block templates from the program, it is necessary to understand the two AutoCAD environments, namely Model and Layout.

7.3.1 Model

The model environment can be recognized by its User Coordinate System (UCS) icon and activated by the Model tab as shown in Figure 7.1. This is the default drawing environment. All geometry constructions, both 2D and 3D, should be performed in this environment.

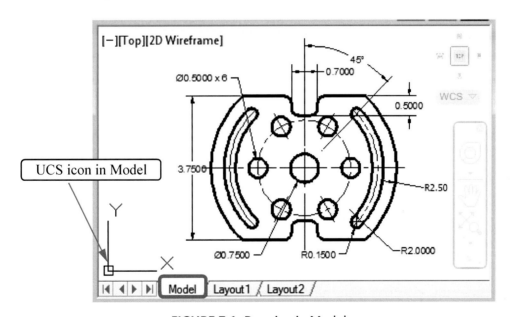

FIGURE 7.1: Drawing in Model

7.3.2 Layout

Although drawings can be created in both environments, the best use for layout is to create multiple views for a single drawing, which cannot be done in the Model environment. Layout is also ideal for a title block because this environment allows the user to zoom the geometry in or out within a standard drawing sheet size without affecting its actual dimensions and without having to scale the title block to match the geometry. Layout can be recognized by its **User Coordinate System** (UCS) icon and can be activated by the Layout tabs as shown in Figure 7.2. By default, a single view (viewport) is created automatically with a layout. It is recommended to remove this view before inserting a title block template because the default view will not provide a good fit to the title block template.

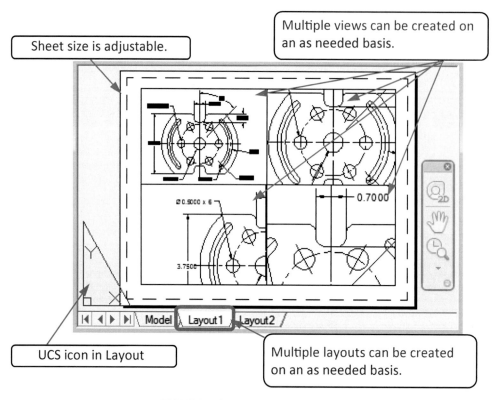

FIGURE 7.2: Drawing in Layout

7.3.3 The general procedures to setup a title block in a drawing

1. Erase the existing viewport from the Layout environment.

    a. Click on a _Layout tab_ to activate the Layout.

    b. Click on the edge of the viewport as shown.

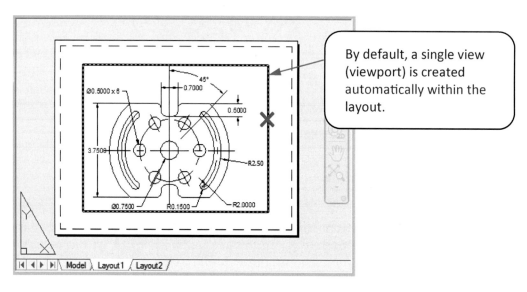

Note: If the view selection is not allowed, it is because the drawing view is active. Double click anywhere outside the viewport to deactivate the drawing view and repeat Step b.

   c.   Press the "**Delete**" button on the keyboard to remove the default viewport.

2.   Insert a title block in the Layout environment.

   a.   Stay in the Layout.

   b.   Enter **MVSETUP** in the Command Line Window.

   c.   Type **T** and press "**Enter**" or select "**Title block**".

   d.   Type **I** and press "**Enter**" or select "**Insert**".

   e.   Select the proper sheet size by entering a number between 0 and 13 and press "Enter". (Enter 9 in this example.)

```
Available title blocks:...
  0:      None
  1:      ISO A4 Size(mm)
  2:      ISO A3 Size(mm)
  3:      ISO A2 Size(mm)
  4:      ISO A1 Size(mm)
  5:      ISO A0 Size(mm)
  6:      ANSI-V Size(in)
  7:      ANSI-A Size(in)
  8:      ANSI-B Size(in)
  9:      ANSI-C Size(in)
 10:       ANSI-D Size(in)
 11:       ANSI-E Size(in)
 12:       Arch/Engineering (24 x 36in)
 13:       Generic D size Sheet (24 x 36in)
```

3.   Insert and fit a drawing view(s) onto a title block inside the Layout environment.

   a.   Insert a Title block in the Layout.

   b.   Select "**Polygonal**" from the Layout Viewports panel in the <u>Layout tab</u>.

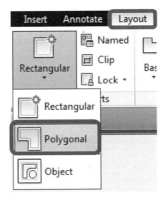

c.   Click on the following steps.

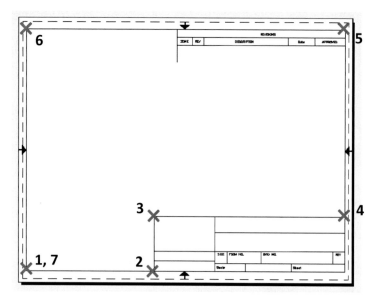

d.   Press "**Enter**" on the keyboard to complete the command.

Note: The drawing view can be activated by double clicking inside the view and deactivated by double clicking outside the view.

4.   Adjust layout (sheet) size

a.   Select "**Page Setup Manager**" from the <u>Output tab</u>.

b.   Choose the layout that needs to be modified and select "**Modify**".

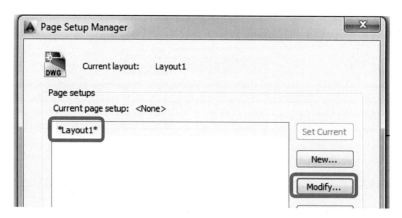

c.   Select proper paper size for the drawing. Then click "**OK**".

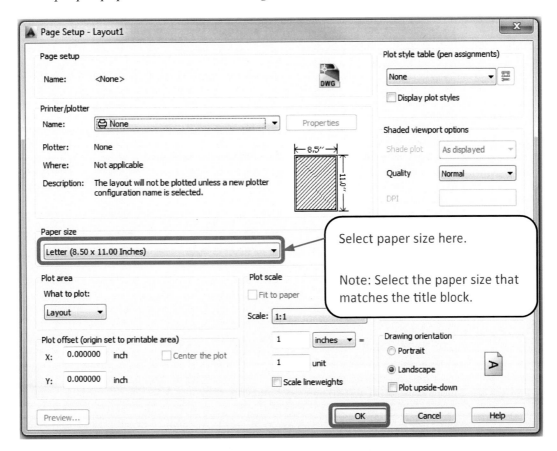

7.4 PLOTTING

There are several plotting options in AutoCAD. Improper use of plotting options will result in unacceptable drawings in paper. This section shows the users how to plot drawings and how to use the plotting options properly.

7.4.1 How to print drawings

1.   Select "**Plot**" from the Output tab.

a.   Specify printer/plotter's name.
b.   Specify paper size.

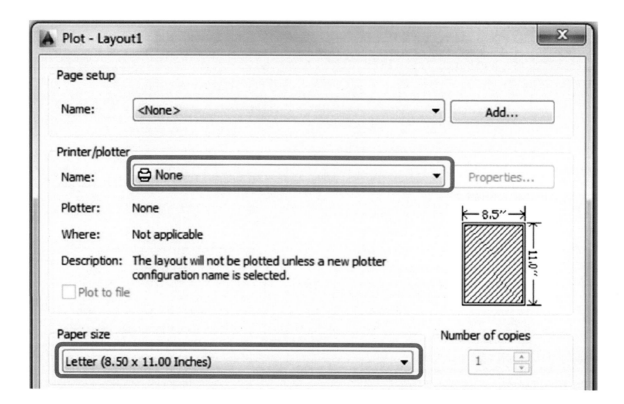

c. Specify Plot area. (**See notes for Plot area options**).

d. Specify Plot scale. (**See notes for Plot scale options**).

e. Select "**Preview**" to preview the drawing output.

f. Click "**OK**" to accept.

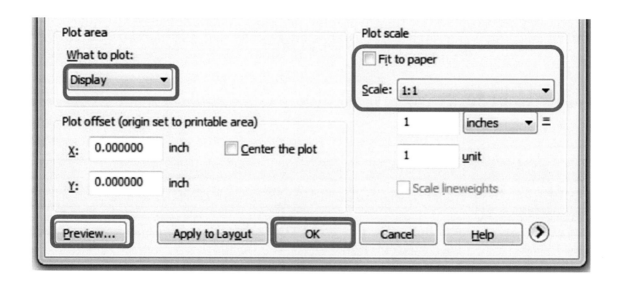

Notes for Plot area options:

Plot area options control the plotting area in the drawing. The four options are:

Display – Only objects displayed on the screen will be plotted.

Extents – Objects within the entire drawing area will be plotted.

Layouts –The entire layout will be plotted.

Window – When this option is chosen, pick two points, forming a window in the drawing. Everything within that window will be plotted.

Notes for Plot scale options:

Plot scale options control the drawing scale on the paper. Users can plot their drawings in different plotting scales.

Fit to paper – This option allows users to plot large objects on small paper size or small objects on large paper size. For example, when plotting 17" x 22" drawing onto a letter size paper (8.5" x 11"), the user does not need to calculate the scale down factor for the drawing. By using this option, drawings will be scaled to the paper size accordingly.

Scale – Drawings can be scaled up or down depending on the scale. For example, if the scale is set to 2:1, the drawing will be two times larger when printed.

Note: The combination of **Window** in Plot area and **Fit to paper** in Plot scale are often used to print large objects on smaller size papers.

DRAW AND TEXT COMMANDS

Two dimensional technical drawings for many engineering applications are generally composed of lines, arcs, circles, rectangles, and texts. These objects can be accurately created using the Draw and Text commands in AutoCAD. Being proficient in these commands is the first step to master the software program. Draw and Text commands are relatively easy to remember and use. The command names correspond to their actual name in English words such as LINE, CIRCLE, and RECTANGLE. Also, the application procedures for these commands are properly guided by simple prompts.

Draw commands are grouped in the Draw panel of the Home tab and Text commands are grouped in the Annotation panel of the same tab as shown in Figure 8.1. These commands are essential for all geometry constructions. As mentioned in Chapter 6, these commands can be executed by clicking on the icons located on the Ribbon, or by entering them in the Command Line Window. In both methods, users must pay high attention to the Command Line Window because it prompts the required steps to execute each command. It will help the users complete their commands successfully.

The lessons covered in this chapter demonstrate how to apply some of the most frequently used Draw commands in absolute and relative coordinate systems. By completing these lessons, new AutoCAD users can quickly manage the basics of the program.

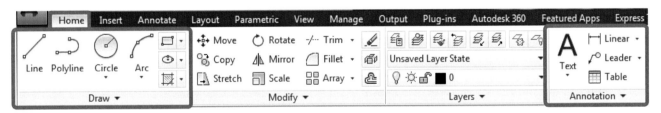

FIGURE 8.1: Draw and Text commands

8.1 TYPES OF DRAW AND TEXT COMMANDS

Types of Draw commands and their application requirements

Draw commands			Basic application requirements
Keyboard	Short-cut	Icon	
			Any of the following
LINE	L	/	» Two points
			» A point and the length of line

Draw commands			Basic application requirements
Keyboard	Short-cut	Icon	
CIRCLE	C		Any of the following » A center point and a radius/diameter » Three points » Two points » Two tangential points and a radius
RECTANGLE	RECTANG		Two points
ARC	A		Any of the following » Three points » Two Points and an angle » Two Points and a radius » Two Points and a chord length » Two Points and a direction » The most effective way to create arcs is to trim circles into arcs because circles are relatively easy to create. Trim command will be introduced in Chapter 10.
POLYGON	POL		Number of sides, a center point, and a radius
ELLIPSE	EL		A point/center point, and two axis lengths
POLYLINE	PLINE		A series of points
HATCH	H		A closed loop geometry

Types of Text commands and their application requirements

Text commands			Basic application requirements
Keyboard	Short-cut	Icon	
Multilinetext	MTEXT or T	A	» Two points
TEXT	TEXT	A	» Starting point » Text height » Rotation angle

8.2 ORTHOGONAL LOCKING

Line command is one of the most frequently used commands in geometry constructions. Besides using coordinates to specify lines, the Ortho command restricts the cursor's movement in horizontal and vertical directions, providing convenience and precision to create horizontal and vertical lines.

Ortho off	Ortho on
The second point of the line will follow the cursor.	The second point of the line will follow the cursor only **horizontally** or **vertically**.

Ortho mode can be toggled on and off by pressing the function key "**F8**" on the keyboard or by clicking on its icon in the status bar as shown.

8.3 SPECIAL SECTION: IMPORTANT NOTES FOR THE LESSONS

Before working on the lessons in this book, it is important to read this section to understanding how the lessons are formatted and laid out.

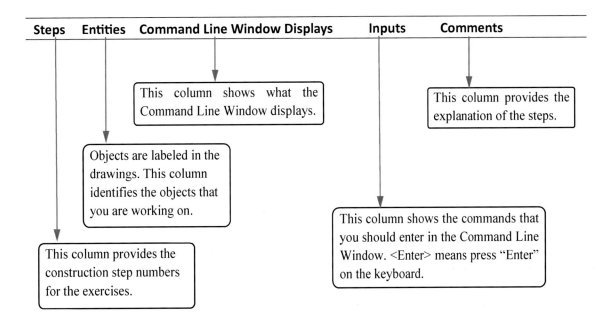

Lesson 1

Create the 2D drawing as shown using the commands listed below.

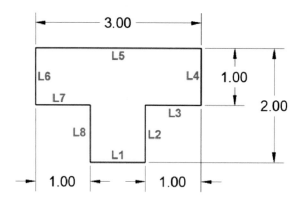

Commands used in this lesson

» Function key "**F12**" (Toggle Dynamic Input on/off)

» Function key "**F8**" (Toggle Ortho on/off)

» **Line**

Method 1 (Absolute coordinates)

Steps	Entities	Command Line Display	Inputs	Comments
1		Type a command	**F12** (Function key)	Dynamic Input <Off> (Ensure its icon is disabled.)

If Dynamic Input icon is not shown, see Relative coordinates under section 6.5.3.

Steps	Entities	Command Line Display	Inputs	Comments
2	L1	Type a command	line <Enter>	Enter Line command.
3		Specify first point:	**1,0** <Enter>	Enter X,Y coordinates.
4		Specify next point or [Undo]:	**2,0** <Enter>	
5	L2	Specify next point or [Undo]:	**2,1** <Enter>	
6	L3	Specify next point or [Close/Undo]:	**3,1** <Enter>	
7	L4	Specify next point or [Close/Undo]:	**3,2** <Enter>	
8	L5	Specify next point or [Close/Undo]:	**0,2** <Enter>	
9	L6	Specify next point or [Close/Undo]:	**0,1** <Enter>	
10	L7	Specify next point or [Close/Undo]:	**1,1** <Enter>	
11	L8	Specify next point or [Close/Undo]:	**1,0** <Enter>	
12		Specify next point or [Close/Undo]:	<Enter>	Finish Line command.

Method 2 (Relative coordinates)

Steps	Entities	Command Line Display	Inputs	Comments
1		Type a command	F12 (Function key)	Dynamic Input <On> (Ensure its icon is enabled.)

MODEL ▦ ▦ ▾ [+▭] ∟ ⊘ ▾ ⋋ ▾ ∠ ◻ ▾ ☰ ▾ ⚙ ▾ + ● ⧉ ⤢ ☰

Steps	Entities	Command Line Display	Inputs	Comments
2	L1	Type a command	**line** <Enter>	Enter Line command.
3		Specify first point:	**1,0** <Enter>	Enter X,Y coordinates.
4		Specify next point or [Undo]:	**1,0** <Enter>	
5	L2	Specify next point or [Undo]:	**0,1** <Enter>	
6	L3	Specify next point or [Close/Undo]:	**1,0** <Enter>	
7	L4	Specify next point or [Close/Undo]:	**0,1** <Enter>	
8	L5	Specify next point or [Close/Undo]:	**-3,0** <Enter>	
9	L6	Specify next point or [Close/Undo]:	**0,-1** <Enter>	
10	L7	Specify next point or [Close/Undo]:	**1,0** <Enter>	
11	L8	Specify next point or [Close/Undo]:	**0,-1** <Enter>	
12		Specify next point or [Close/Undo]:	Esc	Terminate Line command.

Method 3 (Absolute or Relative coordinates)

Steps	Entities	Command Line Display	Inputs	Comments
1		Type a command	F12 (Function key)	Dynamic Input <On or off> (Its icon can be enabled or disabled.)
2		Type a command	F8 (Function key)	Ortho <on> (Ensure its icon is enabled.)

MODEL ▦ ▦ ▾ +▭ [∟] ⊘ ▾ ⋋ ▾ ∠ ◻ ▾ ☰ ▾ ⚙ ▾ + ● ⧉ ⤢ ☰

Steps	Entities	Command Line Display	Inputs	Comments
3	L1	Type a command	**line** <Enter>	Enter Line command.
4		Specify first point:	**1,0** <Enter>	Enter X,Y coordinates.
5		Specify next point or [Undo]:	Move the cursor to the right, type **1** <Enter>	Specify line direction & its length.
6	L2	Specify next point or [Undo]:	Move the cursor upward, type **1** <Enter>	

Steps	Entities	Command Line Display	Inputs	Comments
7	L3	Specify next point or [Close/Undo]:	Move the cursor to the right, type **1** <Enter>	
8	L4	Specify next point or [Close/Undo]:	Move the cursor upward, type **1** <Enter>	
9	L5	Specify next point or [Close/Undo]:	Move the cursor to the left, type **3** <Enter>	
10	L6	Specify next point or [Close/Undo]:	Move the cursor downward, type **1** <Enter>	
11	L7	Specify next point or [Close/Undo]:	Move the cursor to the right, type **1** <Enter>	
12	L8	Specify next point or [Close/Undo]:	**c** <Enter>	Close the loop & finish Line command.

Lesson 2

Create the 2D drawing as shown, using the commands listed below.

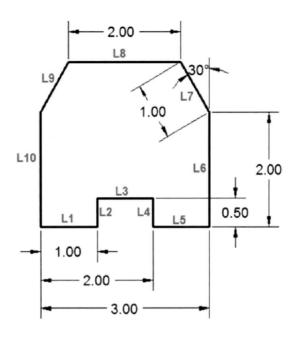

Commands used in this lesson

» Function key "**F12**" (Toggle Dynamic Input on/off)

» Function key "**F8**" (Toggle Ortho on/off)

» **Line**

Method 1 (Absolute coordinates)

Steps	Entities	Command Line Display	Inputs	Comments
1		Type a command	**F12** (Function key)	Dynamic Input <Off> (Ensure its icon is disabled)
		MODEL		
2		Type a command	**F8** (Function key)	Ortho <On> (Ensure its icon is enabled)
		MODEL		
3	L1	Command:	**line** <Enter>	Enter Line command.
4		Specify first point:	**0,0** <Enter>	Enter X,Y coordinates.
5		Specify next point or [Undo]:	**1,0** <Enter>	
6	L2	Specify next point or [Undo]:	**1,0.5** <Enter>	

Steps	Entities	Command Line Display	Inputs	Comments
7	L3	Specify next point or [Close/Undo]:	**2,0.5** <Enter>	
8	L4	Specify next point or [Close/Undo]:	**2,0** <Enter>	
9	L5	Specify next point or [Close/Undo]:	**3,0** <Enter>	
10	L6	Specify next point or [Close/Undo]:	**3,2** <Enter>	
11	L7	Specify next point or [Close/Undo]:	**3.8<49** <Enter>	In absolute mode, this point is 3.8" away from the origin and 49° from the X axis.

Steps	Entities	Command Line Display	Inputs	Comments
12	L8	Specify next point or [Close/Undo]:	Move the cursor to the left, type **2** <Enter>	Use this method to avoid calculations.
13	L9	Specify next point or [Close/Undo]:	**0,2** <Enter>	
14	L10	Specify next point or [Close/Undo]:	**c** <Enter>	Close the loop & finish Line command.

Method 2 (Relative coordinates)

Steps	Entities	Command Line Display	Inputs	Comments
1		Type a command	**F12** (Function key)	Dynamic Input <On> (Ensure its icon is enabled.)
		MODEL ▦ ▦ ▾ ⊞ ∟ ☉ ▾ ✕ ▾ ∠ ☐ ▾ ☰ ▾ ⚙ ▾ ✛ ● ⌗ ⬈ ≡		
2	L1	Type a command	**line** <Enter>	Enter Line command.
3		Specify first point:	<Click anywhere within the Graphics Window>	Start from a random point.
4		Specify next point or [Undo]:	**1,0** <Enter>	Enter X,Y coordinates based on relative coordination system.
5	L2	Specify next point or [Undo]:	**0,0.5** <Enter>	
6	L3	Specify next point or [Close/Undo]:	**1,0** <Enter>	
7	L4	Specify next point or [Close/Undo]:	**0,-0.5** <Enter>	
8	L5	Specify next point or [Close/Undo]:	**1,0** <Enter>	
9	L6	Specify next point or [Close/Undo]:	**0,2** <Enter>	
10	L7	Specify next point or [Close/Undo]:	**1<120** <Enter>	The point is 1″ away from the last point and 120° from X axis.
11	L8	Specify next point or [Close/Undo]:	**-2,0** <Enter>	
12	L9	Specify next point or [Close/Undo]:	**1<240** <Enter>	
13	L10	Specify next point or [Close/Undo]:	**0,-2** <Enter>	
14		Specify next point or [Close/Undo]:	Esc	Terminate Line command.

Method 3 (Absolute mode with temporary relative coordinate activation)

Steps	Entities	Command Line Display	Inputs	Comments
1		Type a command	F12 (Function key)	Dynamic Input <Off> (Ensure its icon is disabled.)
		MODEL ▦ ▦ ▾ ⊞ ⌐ ⊘ ▾ ⤬ ▾ ∠ ▢ ▾ ☰ ▾ ✿ ▾ + ⬤ ⬚ ⬀ ☰		
2	L1	Type a command	**line** <Enter>	Enter Line command.
3		Specify first point:	<Click anywhere within the Graphics Window>	Start from a random point.
4		Specify next point or [Undo]:	**@1,0** <Enter>	Use @ to temporarily activate relative mode while entering X,Y coordinate.
5	L2	Specify next point or [Undo]:	**@0,0.5** <Enter>	
6	L3	Specify next point or [Close/ Undo]:	**@1,0** <Enter>	
7	L4	Specify next point or [Close/ Undo]:	**@0,-0.5** <Enter>	
8	L5	Specify next point or [Close/ Undo]:	**@1,0** <Enter>	
9	L6	Specify next point or [Close/ Undo]:	**@0,2** <Enter>	
10	L7	Specify next point or [Close/ Undo]:	**@1<120** <Enter>	Use @ to temporarily activate relative mode while entering length and angle.
11	L8	Specify next point or [Close/ Undo]:	**@-2,0** <Enter>	
13	L9	Specify next point or [Close/ Undo]:	**@1<240** <Enter>	
14	L10	Specify next point or [Close/ Undo]:	**c** <Enter>	Close the loop & finish the Line command.

Lesson 3

Create the 2D drawing as shown using the commands listed below.

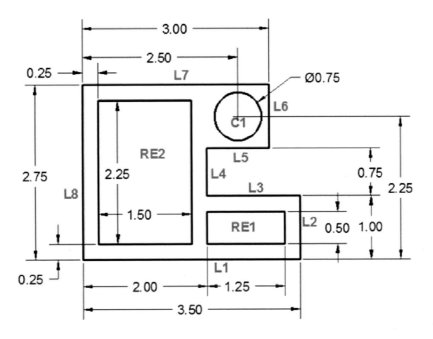

Commands used in this lesson

»   Function key "**F12**" (Toggle Dynamic Input on/off)

»   **Line**

»   **Circle**

»   **Rectangle**

Method 1 (Absolute coordinates)

Steps	Entities	Command Line Display	Inputs	Comments
1		Type a command	**F12** (Function key)	Dynamic Input <Off> (Ensure its icon is disabled.)
		MODEL ▦ ▦ ▾ ⊞ ⌞ ⏚ ▾ ⨯ ▾ ∠ ◻ ▾ ≡ ▾ ❂ ▾ + ⬤ ⧉ ◪ ≡		
2	L1	Type a command	**line** <Enter>	Enter Line command.
3		Specify first point:	**0,0** <Enter>	Enter X,Y coordinates.
4		Specify next point or [Undo]:	**3.5,0** <Enter>	
5	L2	Specify next point or [Undo]:	**3.5,1** <Enter>	
6	L3	Specify next point or [Close/Undo]:	**2,1** <Enter>	
7	L4	Specify next point or [Close/Undo]:	**2,1.75** <Enter>	

Steps	Entities	Command Line Display	Inputs	Comments
8	L5	Specify next point or [Close/Undo]:	**3,1.75** <Enter>	
9	L6	Specify next point or [Close/Undo]:	**3,2.75** <Enter>	
10	L7	Specify next point or [Close/Undo]:	**0,2.75**<Enter>	
11	L8	Specify next point or [Close/Undo]:	**c** <Enter>	Close the loop & finish Line command.
12	RE1	Type a command	**rectangle** <Enter>	Enter Rectangle command.
13		Specify first corner point or [Chamfer/Elevation/Fillet/Thickness/Width]:	**2,0.25** <Enter>	Enter X,Y coordinates of the first corner point.
14		Specify other corner point or [Area/Dimensions/Rotation]:	**3.25,0.75** <Enter>	Enter X,Y coordinates of other corner point.
15	RE2	Type a command	<Enter>	Repeat last command. (Rectangle)
16		Specify first corner point or [Chamfer/Elevation/Fillet/Thickness/Width]:	**0.25,0.25** <Enter>	
17		Specify other corner point or [Area/Dimensions/Rotation]:	**1.75,2.5** <Enter>	
18	C1	Type a command	**circle** <Enter>	Enter Circle command.
19		Specify center point for circle or [3P/2P/Ttr (tan tan radius)]:	**2.5,2.25** <Enter>	Enter X,Y coordinates of the center point.
20		Specify radius of circle or [Diameter]:	**0.375** <Enter>	Enter radius of the circle.

Method 2 (Relative coordinates)

Steps	Entities	Command Line Display	Inputs	Comments
1		Type a command	**F12** (Function key)	Dynamic Input <On> (Ensure its icon is enabled.)
		MODEL ▦ ▦ ▾ ⊞ ∟ ⊘ ▾ ⋋ ▾ ∠ ▢ ▾ ☰ ▾ ⚙ ▾ ＋ ● ⬚ ▨ ≡		
2	L1	Type a command	**line** <Enter>	Enter Line command.
3		Specify first point:	**0,0** <Enter>	Enter X,Y coordinates.
4		Specify next point or [Undo]:	**3.5,0** <Enter>	
5	L2	Specify next point or [Undo]:	**0,1** <Enter>	
6	L3	Specify next point or [Close/ Undo]:	**-1.5,0** <Enter>	
7	L4	Specify next point or [Close/ Undo]:	**0,0.75** <Enter>	
8	L5	Specify next point or [Close/ Undo]:	**1,0** <Enter>	
9	L6	Specify next point or [Close/ Undo]:	**0,1** <Enter>	
10	L7	Specify next point or [Close/ Undo]:	**-3,0** <Enter>	
11	L8	Specify next point or [Close/ Undo]:	**c** <Enter>	Close the loop & finish Line command.
12	RE1	Type a command	**rectangle** <Enter>	Enter Rectangle command.
13		Specify first corner point or [Chamfer/Elevation/Fillet/ Thickness/Width]:	**2,0.25** <Enter>	Enter X,Y coordinates of the first corner point.
16		Specify other corner point or [Area/Dimensions/Rotation]:	**1.25,0.5** <Enter>	Enter X,Y coordinates of other corner point based on relative coordination system.
17	RE2	Type a command	<Enter>	Repeat last command. (Rectangle)
18		Specify first corner point or [Chamfer/Elevation/Fillet/ Thickness/Width]:	**0.25,0.25** <Enter>	
19		Specify other corner point or [Area/Dimensions/Rotation]:	**1.5,2.25** <Enter>	
20	C1	Type a command	**circle** <Enter>	Enter Circle command.
21		Specify center point for circle or [3P/2P/Ttr (tan tan radius)]:	**2.5,2.25** <Enter>	Enter X,Y coordinates of the center point.
22		Specify radius of circle or [Diameter]:	**0.375** <Enter>	Enter radius of the circle.

Lesson 4

Create the 2D drawing as shown using the commands listed below.

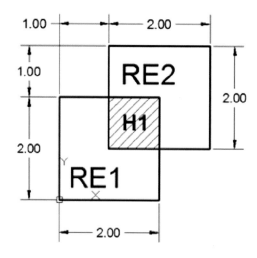

Commands used in this lesson

»   Function key "**F12**" (Toggle Dynamic Input on/off)

»   **Rectangle**

»   **Hatch**

»   **Mtext**

»   **Text**

(Absolute coordinates)

Steps	Entities	Command Line Display	Inputs	Comments
1		Type a command	**F12** (Function key)	Dynamic Input <Off> (Ensure its icon is disabled.)
		MODEL		
2	**RE1**	Type a command	**rectangle** <Enter>	Enter Rectangle command.
3		Specify first corner point or [Chamfer/Elevation/Fillet/Thickness/Width]:	**0,0** <Enter>	Enter X,Y coordinates of the first corner point.
4		Specify other corner point or [Area/Dimensions/Rotation]:	**2,2** <Enter>	Enter X,Y coordinates of other corner point.
5	**RE1**	Type a command	<Enter>	Repeat last command (Rectangle).
6		Specify first corner point or [Chamfer/Elevation/Fillet/Thickness/Width]:	**1,1** <Enter>	

Steps	Entities	Command Line Display	Inputs	Comments
7		Specify other corner point or [Area/Dimensions/Rotation]:	3,3 <Enter>	
8	H1	Type a command	hatch <Enter>	Enter Hatch command.
9		Pick internal point or [objects/ Undo/settings]:	<Select the inside of the small square as shown>	
10		Pick internal point or [objects/ Undo/settings]:	<Enter>	Finish Hatch command. (See notes at the end of this lesson for more explanation on Hatch command.)
11	RE1 (Text)	Type a command	mtext <Enter>	Enter Mtext command.
12		Specify first corner	<Select the open area as shown>	
13		Specify opposite corner or [Height/Justify/Line spacing/ Rotation/Style/Width/ Columns]	h <Enter>	Activate the setting for the height of the text.
14		Specify height <0.2000>:	0.4<Enter>	Enter the height of the text.
15		Specify opposite corner or [Height/Justify/Line spacing/ Rotation/Style/Width/ Columns]	<Select outside the area as shown>	
16			<Type> RE1 and click outside the text box when complete	
17		Use Steps 11 to 16 as reference to create RE2 (Text)		
18	H1 (Text)	Type a command	text <Enter>	Enter text command.

Steps	Entities	Command Line Display	Inputs	Comments
19		Specify start point of text or [Justify/style]:	<Select inside the hatched area as shown>	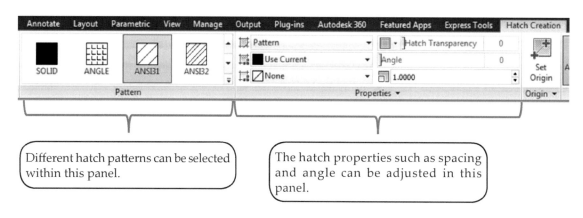
20		Specify height <0.4000>:	0.3<Enter>	Enter the height of the text.
21		Specify rotation angle of text <0>:	<Enter>	Accept the default value.
22			<Type> **H1** and click outside the text box when complete	
23			<Enter>	Finish text command.

Note for **Hatch** command:

Hatch Creation tab will appear after the **Hatch** command is entered. Hatch pattern and properties can be adjusted by the following settings. Once the pattern and properties are defined, press "**Enter**" on the keyboard to end the command.

Different hatch patterns can be selected within this panel.

The hatch properties such as spacing and angle can be adjusted in this panel.

Exercise 8.1

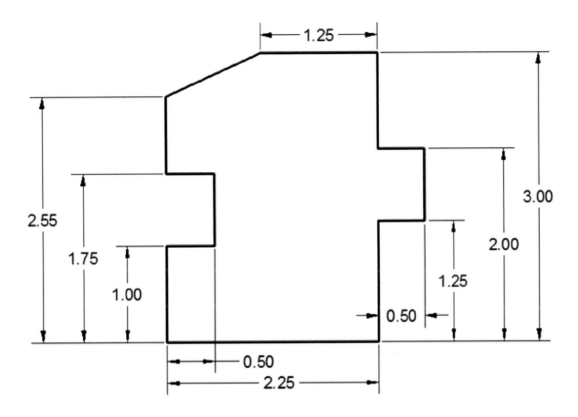

Exercise 8.2

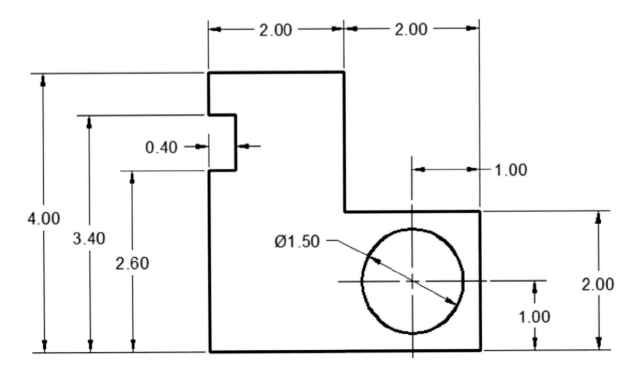

Exercise 8.3

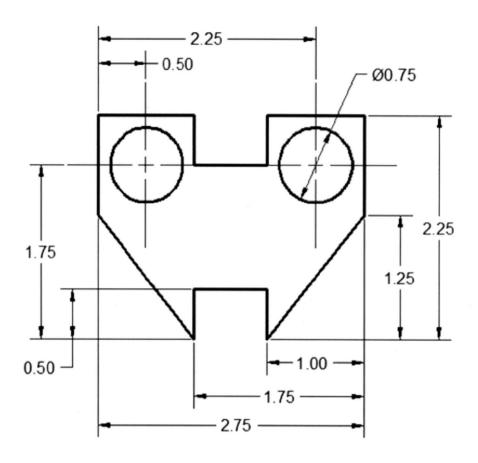

Exercise 8.4

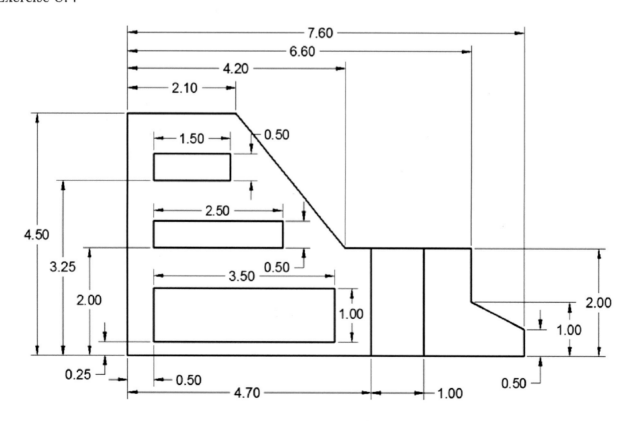

OBJECT SNAPS

Geometries can be created accurately by entering the precise coordinates in the Draw commands. However, in many complex designs, coordinates of objects are not given and not easy to find. Inexperienced AutoCAD users have the tendency of using "good-by-eye" estimation to specify the location of the object or a point. Although coordinates can be acquired using a series of trigonometry calculations, the calculated values may contain many decimal places which will be impractical to enter for each coordinate and drawings will be inaccurate if the coordinates are entered partially.

Object snaps in AutoCAD provide users with an accurate tool to specify a particular point on an object. These commands cannot be used independently for geometry construction, but rather they will be used during a command operation where specific locations are required. Object Snaps are available and can be accessed by the **OSNAP** or **DSETTINGS** commands as shown in Figure 9.1.

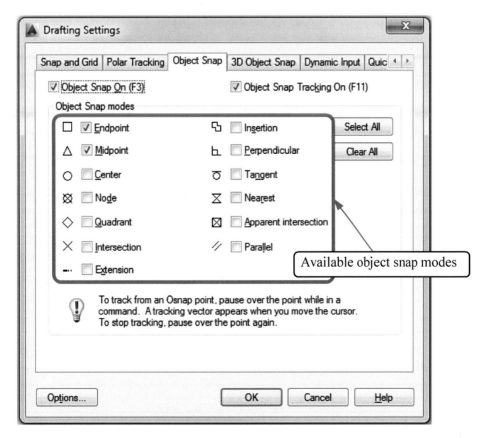

FIGURE 9.1: Object Snap modes

9.1 TYPES OF OBJECT SNAPS AND THEIR FUNCTIONS

Object snap commands				Examples	
Keyboard	Short-cut	Icon	Function	OSNAP mode off	OSNAP mode on
Endpoint	END		Snaps to an endpoint		Endpoint
Midpoint	MID		Snaps to a midpoint		Midpoint
Intersection	INT		Snaps to an intersection point		Intersection
Apparent Intersection	APP		Snaps to a virtual intersection point		Intersection
Extension	EXT		Specifies a point on the extension		Extension: 1.0710 < 194°
Center	CEN		Snaps to a center point		Center
Quadrant	QUA		Snaps to a quadrant point		Quadrant
Tangent	TAN		Snaps to the tangent of arcs, circles, or ellipses		Tangent
Perpendicular	PER		Constrains a new line perpendicular to an object		Perpendicular
Parallel	PAR		Constrains a new line parallel to another line		Parallel 1.5045 < 1
Node	NOD		Snaps to a point		Node

Object snap commands				Examples	
Keyboard	Short-cut	Icon	Function	OSNAP mode off	OSNAP mode on
Insertion	INS		Snaps to a block or text	┼TEXT	TEXT Insert
Nearest	NEA		Snaps the nearest point along the object		Nearest

9.1.1 How to setup and apply Object Snaps

1. Select the appropriate object snap modes. Keep in mind that the selected object snap modes will not be active until Object Snap is enabled (Step 2).

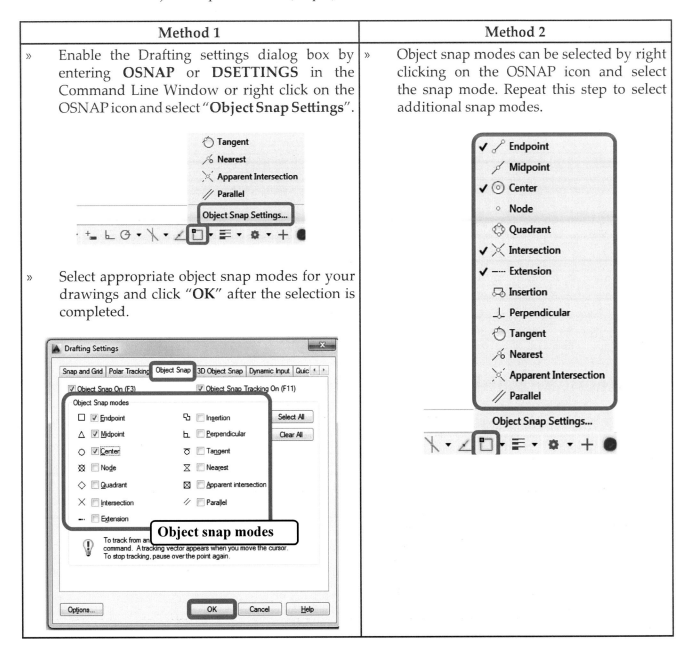

Method 1	Method 2
» Enable the Drafting settings dialog box by entering **OSNAP** or **DSETTINGS** in the Command Line Window or right click on the OSNAP icon and select "**Object Snap Settings**".	» Object snap modes can be selected by right clicking on the OSNAP icon and select the snap mode. Repeat this step to select additional snap modes.
» Select appropriate object snap modes for your drawings and click "**OK**" after the selection is completed.	

2. Enable and disable Object Snap when necessary.

Object Snap can be toggled on and off by pressing the function key "**F3**" on the keyboard or by clicking on its icon in the Status Bar as shown.

3. Override preset object snaps with a specific object snap when necessary.

Method 1	Method 2
During a command operation, enter the object snap command or short-cut (e.g. END, INT, MID, CEN) in the Command Line Window. (Note: Commands are NOT case sensitive. See Section 9.1 for short-cuts of object snap commands.)	During a command operation, right click in the Graphics Window, select Snap Overrides, and then select the necessary object snap commands.

Note: It is not recommended to activate all object snap modes because selection of location will be difficult in small areas.

9.2 SELECTION TECHNIQUES

Similar to many Microsoft applications, objects can be selected by making a selection window around the objects. In AutoCAD, creating a selection window in different directions will result in different selection options. The examples below demonstrate the difference between window and crossing selections.

Window selection	Crossing selection
When creating the window from left (point 1) to right (point 2), the window is displayed in solid lines. Only objects inside the window will be selected. In this example, only the circle is selected.	When creating the window from right (point 1) to left (point 2), the window is displayed in dashed lines. Everything inside or intersecting with the window will be selected. In this example, both the line and the circle are selected.

9.3 GRID DISPLAY

A grid can be displayed as a background of the graphics window. It provides a visual reference for geometry construction and it does not show up on the paper when printing the drawing. Figure 8.2 shows examples of two drawings with and without grid display.

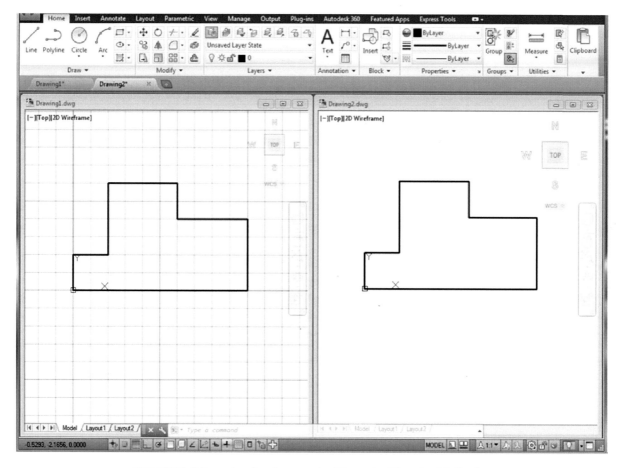

FIGURE 8.2 Drawing background with and without grid display

Grid display can be toggled on and off by pressing the function key **"F7"** on the keyboard or by clicking on its icon in the status bar as shown.

9.3.1 How to adjust grid display

1.   Enter **DSETTINGS** in the command line and select the Snap and Grid tab (or Right click on the SNAPMODE icon and select "**Snap Settings**".)

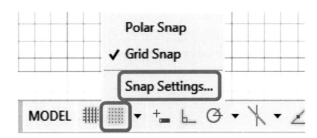

2.   Change the values of the Grid spacing according to the needs.

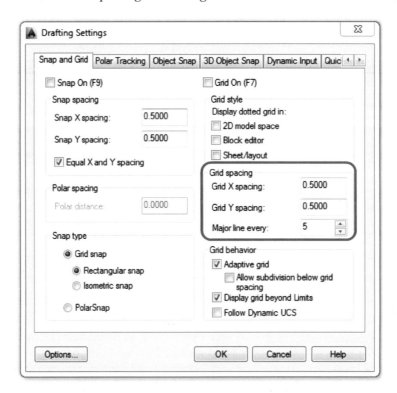

Lesson 5 — Part 1

Create the 2D drawing as shown using the commands listed below.

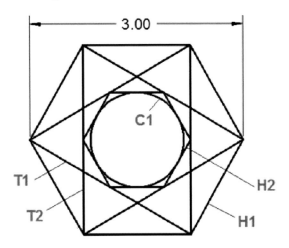

Commands used in this lesson

» Function key "**F3**" (Toggle Osnap <Object Snap> on/off)

» Function key "**F7**" (Toggle Grid Display on/off)

» **Osnap**

» **Polygon**

» **Line**

» **Circle (3P)**

Method 1 (OSNAP Off)

Steps	Entities	Command Line Display	Inputs	Comments
1		Type a command	F3 (Function key)	Osnap <Off> (Ensure its icon is disabled.)
		MODEL ▦ ▦ ▾ +ₗ ∟ ⊙ ▾ ✕ ▾ ∠ ▣ ▾ ☰ ▾ ✿ ▾ + ● ⏹ ↗ ☰		
2		Type a command	F7 (Function key)	Grid display <Off> (Ensure its icon is disabled.)
		MODEL ▦ ▦ ▾ +ₗ ∟ ⊙ ▾ ✕ ▾ ∠ ▣ ▾ ☰ ▾ ✿ ▾ + ● ⏹ ↗ ☰		
3	H1	Type a command	polygon <Enter>	Enter Polygon command.
4		Enter number of sides <4>:	**6** <Enter>	Enter six sides for hexagon.
5		Specify center of polygon or [Edge]:	<Click anywhere within the graphics window>	Start from a random point.

Steps	Entities	Command Line Display	Inputs	Comments
6		Enter an option [Inscribed in circle Circumscribed about circle] <I>:	I <Enter>	Hexagon inside an imaginary circle.
7		Specify radius of circle:	1.5 <Enter>	Enter radius of the imaginary circle.
8	T1	Type a command	line <Enter>	Enter Line command.
9		Specify first point:	end <Enter>	Activate endpoint snap.
10		of	<Select the corner as shown>	
11		Specify next point or [Undo]:	end <Enter>	
12		of	<Select the corner as shown>	
13		Specify next point or [Undo]:	end <Enter>	
14		of	<Select the corner as shown>	
15		Specify next point or [Close/Undo]:	end <Enter>	
16		of	<Select the first corner >	
17		Specify next point or [Close/Undo]:	<Enter>	Finish Line command.
18	T2	Type a command	<Enter>	Repeat last command. (Line)
19		Specify first point:	end <Enter>	Activate endpoint snap.
20		of	<Select the corner as shown>	
21		Specify next point or [Undo]:	end <Enter>	
22		of	<Select the corner as shown>	
23		Specify next point or [Undo]:	end <Enter>	
24		of	<Select the corner as shown>	

Steps	Entities	Command Line Display	Inputs	Comments
25		Specify next point or [Close/Undo]:	**end** \<Enter\>	
26		of	\<Select the corner as shown\>	
27		Specify next point or [Close/Undo]:	\<Enter\>	Finish Line command.
28	H2	Type a command	\<Enter\>	Repeat last command. (Line)
29		Specify first point:	**mid** \<Enter\>	Activate midpoint snap.
30		of	\<Select the midpoint as shown\>	
31		Repeat Step 29 for the midpoints 1 – 6 as shown		
32		Specify next point or [Close/Undo]:	\<Enter\>	Finish Line command.
33	C1	Type a command	**circle** \<Enter\>	Enter circle command.
34		Specify center point for circle or [3P/2P/Ttr (tan tan radius)]:	**3P** \<Enter\>	Activate "3 points" option.
35		Specify first point on circle:	**mid** \<Enter\>	Activate midpoint snap.
36		of	\<Select the midpoint as shown\>	
37		Repeat Step 35 for the midpoints 1 & 2 as shown.		

Method 2 (OSNAP On)

Steps	Entities	Command Line Display	Inputs	Comments
1		Type a command	F3 (Function key)	Osnap <On>, (Ensure this icon is enabled.)

MODEL ▦ ▦ ▾ +̲ ∟ ⊘ ▾ ✕ ▾ ⊿ ⬚ ▾ ☰ ▾ ⚙ ▾ + ● ⬚ ⤢ ☰

Steps	Entities	Command Line Display	Inputs	Comments
2		Type a command	Osnap <Enter>	

Activate only **Endpoint** and **Midpoint** object snap modes and then click "**OK**".

Steps	Entities	Command Line Display	Inputs	Comments
3	H1	Type a command	polygon <Enter>	Enter Polygon command.
4		Enter number of sides <4>:	6 <Enter>	Enter six sides for hexagon.
5		Specify center of polygon or [Edge]:	<**Click** anywhere within the graphic window>	Start from a random point.
6		Enter an option [Inscribed in circle Circumscribed about circle] <I>:	I <Enter>	Hexagon inside an imaginary circle.
7		Specify radius of circle:	1.5 <Enter>	Enter radius of the imaginary circle.
8	T1	Type a command	line <Enter>	Enter Line command.

Steps	Entities	Command Line Display	Inputs	Comments
9		Specify first point:	<Click on the following steps>	
10		Specify next point or [Close/Undo]:	<Enter>	Finish Line command.
11	T2	Type a command	<Enter>	Repeat last command. (Line)
12		Specify first point:	<Click on the following steps>	
13		Specify next point or [Close/Undo]:	<Enter>	Finish Line command.
14	H2	Type a command	<Enter>	Repeat last command. (Line)
15		Specify next point or [Close/Undo]:	<Click on the following steps>	
16		Specify next point or [Close/Undo]:	<Enter>	Finish Line command.
17	C1	Type a command	**circle** <Enter>	Enter circle command.
18		Specify center point for circle or [3P/2P/Ttr (tan tan radius)]:	**3P** <Enter>	Activate "3 points" option.

Steps	Entities	Command Line Display	Inputs	Comments
19		Specify first point on circle:	\<Click on the following steps\>	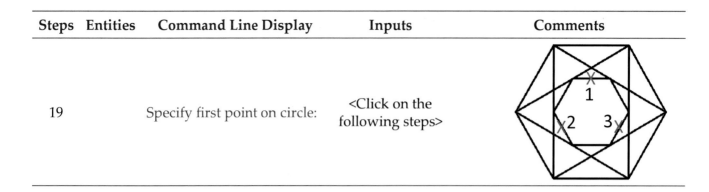

Method 3 (OSNAP On – All object snap modes are active)

Repeat Method 2 with the following settings on the OSNAP dialog box to determine which way is easier to use.

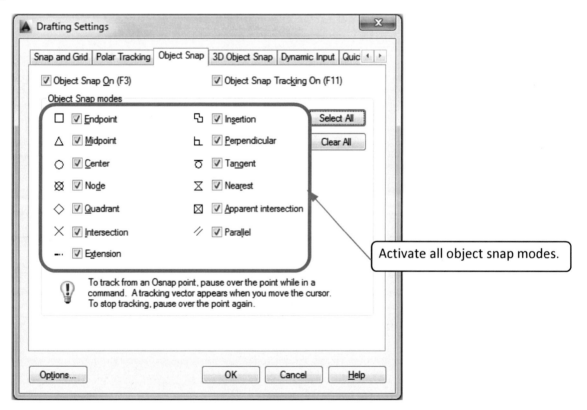

Lesson 5 – Part 2 (Selection techniques)

Commands used in this lesson

» **Delete**

» **Undo**

» Selection techniques
>> Window selection
>> Crossing selection

Steps	Entities	Command Line Display	Inputs	Comments
1		Type a command	<Click on the following steps>	Make a window selection.
				The window must be smaller than the large hexagon but larger than the small hexagon.
2		Type a command	Press <Delete> on the keyboard	This will delete the small hexagon and the circle.
3		Type a command	**UNDO** <Enter>	Undo delete command.
4		Type a command	<Click on the following steps>	Make a crossing selection.
				The window must be smaller than the large hexagon but larger than the small hexagon.
5		Type a command	Press <Delete> on the keyboard	This will delete everything.

NOTE: If the "**Delete**" button on the Keyboard does not delete objects, enter PICKFIRST in the command line and set the variable to 1.

Lesson 6

Create the 2D drawing as shown using the commands listed below.

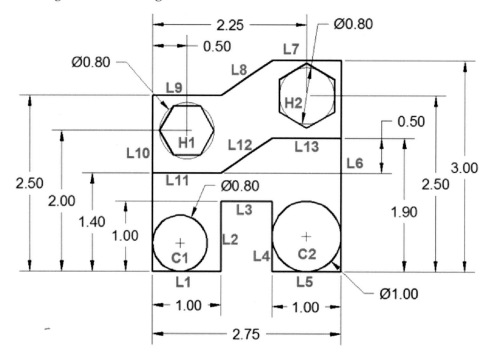

Commands used in this lesson

» Function key "**F12**" (Toggle Dynamic Input on/off)

» Function key "**F8**" (Toggle Ortho on/off)

» Function key "**F3**" (Toggle Osnap <Object Snap> On/off)

» **Line**

» **Circle (TTR & 3P)**

» **UCS**

» **Polygon**

Steps	Entities	Command Line Display	Inputs	Comments
1		Type a command	**F12** (Function key)	Dynamic Input <On> (Ensure its icon is enabled.)
		MODEL ▦ ▤ ▾ [+□] L ⊙ ▾ ⋋ ▾ ∠ □ ▾ ☰ ▾ ✿ ▾ + ● 😐 ⟐ ☰		
2			**F8** (Function key)	Ortho <On> (Ensure its icon is enabled.)
		MODEL ▦ ▤ ▾ +□ [L] ⊙ ▾ ⋋ ▾ ∠ □ ▾ ☰ ▾ ✿ ▾ + ● 😐 ⟐ ☰		
3		Type a command	F3 (Function key)	Osnap <On> (Ensure its icon is enabled.)
		MODEL ▦ ▤ ▾ +□ L ⊙ ▾ ⋋ ▾ ∠ [□] ▾ ☰ ▾ ✿ ▾ + ● 😐 ⟐ ☰		

Steps	Entities	Command Line Display	Inputs	Comments
4		Type a command	**Osnap** <Enter>	

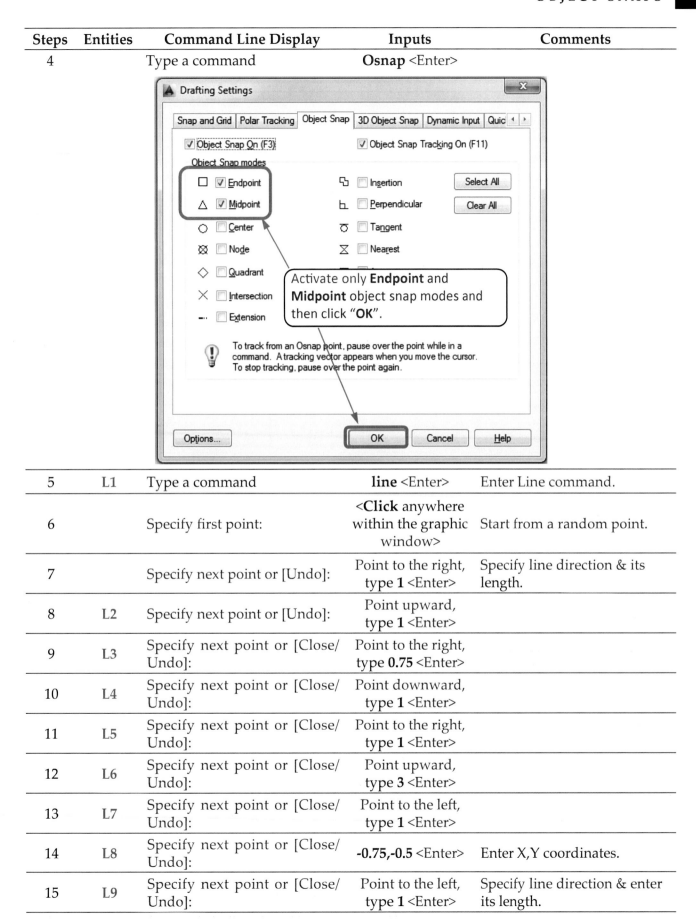

Activate only **Endpoint** and **Midpoint** object snap modes and then click "**OK**".

Steps	Entities	Command Line Display	Inputs	Comments
5	L1	Type a command	**line** <Enter>	Enter Line command.
6		Specify first point:	<**Click** anywhere within the graphic window>	Start from a random point.
7		Specify next point or [Undo]:	Point to the right, type **1** <Enter>	Specify line direction & its length.
8	L2	Specify next point or [Undo]:	Point upward, type **1** <Enter>	
9	L3	Specify next point or [Close/Undo]:	Point to the right, type **0.75** <Enter>	
10	L4	Specify next point or [Close/Undo]:	Point downward, type **1** <Enter>	
11	L5	Specify next point or [Close/Undo]:	Point to the right, type **1** <Enter>	
12	L6	Specify next point or [Close/Undo]:	Point upward, type **3** <Enter>	
13	L7	Specify next point or [Close/Undo]:	Point to the left, type **1** <Enter>	
14	L8	Specify next point or [Close/Undo]:	**-0.75,-0.5** <Enter>	Enter X,Y coordinates.
15	L9	Specify next point or [Close/Undo]:	Point to the left, type **1** <Enter>	Specify line direction & enter its length.

Steps	Entities	Command Line Display	Inputs	Comments
16	L10	Specify next point or [Close/Undo]:	<Select the end of line **L1**>	

17		Specify next point or [Close/Undo]:	<Enter>	Finish Line command.
18		Type a command	**ucs** <Enter>	Set User Coordinate System.
19		Specify origin of UCS:	<Select the end of line **L10**>	Set end point of L10 as origin.

20		Specify origin on X-axis or <accept>:	<Enter>	Accept & finish the UCS command.
21	L11	Type a command	**line** <Enter>	Enter Line command.
22		Specify first point:	**0,1.4** <Enter>	
23		Specify next point or [Close/Undo]:	Point to the right, type 1<Enter>	
24	L12	Specify next point or [Close/Undo]:	**0.75,0.5**<Enter>	
25	L13	Specify next point or [Close/Undo]:	Point to the right, type 1<Enter>	
26		Specify next point or [Close/Undo]:	Esc	Terminate line command.
27	C1	Type a command	**circle** <Enter>	Enter circle command.
28		Specify center point for circle or [3P/2P/Ttr (tan tan radius)]:	**ttr** <Enter>	Activate "tan tan radius" option.
29		Specify point on object for first tangent of circle:	<Select line **L1**>	
		Specify point on object for second tangent of circle:	<Select line **L10**>	

| 30 | | Specify radius of circle: | **0.4**<Enter> | Enter radius of circle. |
| 31 | C2 | Type a command | <Enter> | Repeat last command. (circle) |

Steps	Entities	Command Line Display	Inputs	Comments
32		Specify center point for circle or [3P/2P/Ttr (tan tan radius)]:	**3P** <Enter>	Activate "3 points" option.
33		Specify first point on circle:	**tan** <Enter>	Activate tangent snap.
34		to	<Select line **L4**>	
35		Specify second point on circle:	**tan** <Enter>	
36		to	<Select line **L5**>	
37		Specify third point on circle:	**tan** <Enter>	
38		to	<Select line **L6**>	
39	H1	Type a command	**polygon** <Enter>	Enter Polygon command.
40		Enter number of sides <4>:	**6** <Enter>	Enter six sides for hexagon.
41		Specify center of polygon or [Edge]:	**0.5,2** <Enter>	Enter X,Y coordinate.
42		Enter an option [Inscribed in circle Circumscribed about circle] <I>:	**I**<Enter>	Hexagon inside an imaginary circle.
43		Specify radius of circle:	**0.4**<Enter>	Enter radius of the imaginary circle.
44	H2	Type a command	<Enter>	Repeat last command. (polygon)
45		Enter number of sides <4>:	**6** <Enter>	
46		Specify center of polygon or [Edge]:	**2.25,2.5** <Enter>	
47		Enter an option [Inscribed in circle Circumscribed about circle] <I>:	**c**<Enter>	Hexagon outside an imaginary circle.
48		Specify radius of circle:	**0.4**<Enter>	

Exercise 9.1

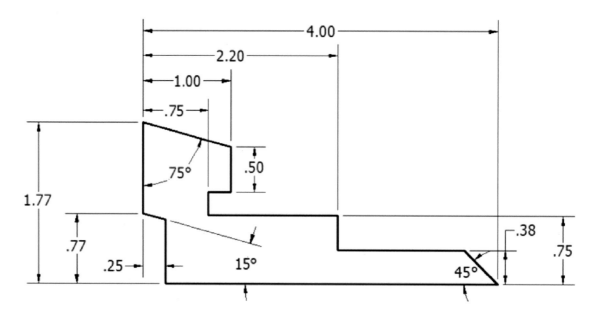

Exercise 9.2

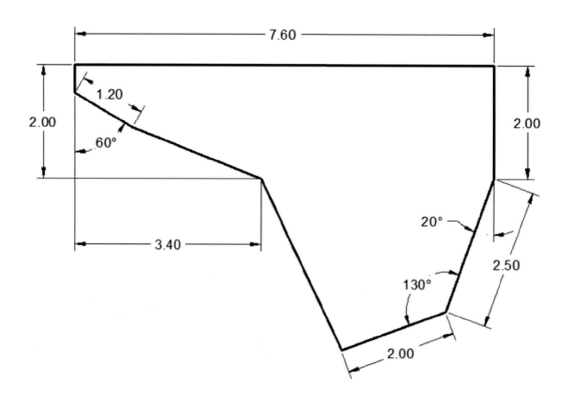

Exercise 9.3

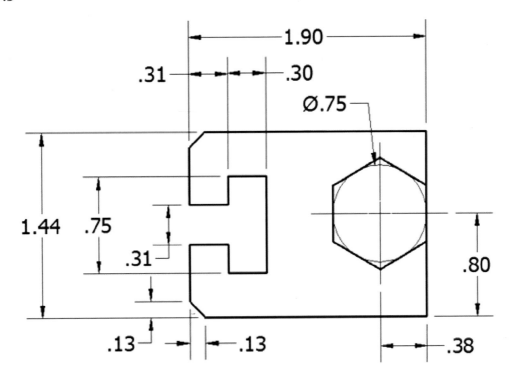

Exercise 9.4

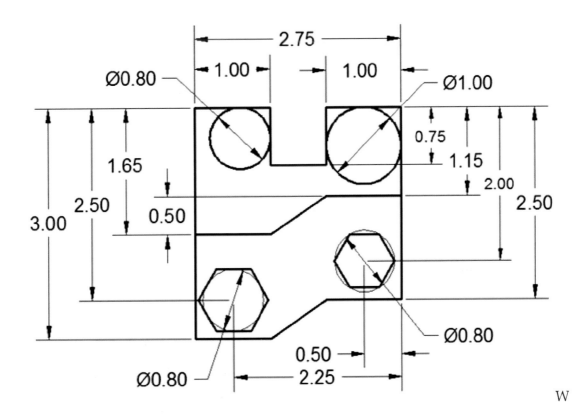

W

MODIFY COMMANDS

AutoCAD has a set of modify commands that enhance the use of draw commands. Modify commands allow users to modify existing objects to the required shapes where coordinates of the points are impractical to obtain. Modify commands are grouped in the modify panel of the home tab as shown in Figure 10.1. Similar to Draw commands, Modify commands can be executed by clicking on the icons located on the Ribbon, or by entering them in the Command Line Window. Users must pay high attention to the Command Line Window because it prompts the required steps for each executed command.

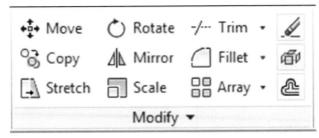

FIGURE 10.1: Modify commands

10.1 TYPES OF MODIFY COMMANDS

Modify commands			Examples	Examples
Keyboard	Short-cut	Icon	(Before application)	(After application)
Move	M			
Copy	CO			
Stretch	Stretch			

| Modify commands | | | Examples | Examples |
Keyboard	Short-cut	Icon	(Before application)	(After application)
Rotate	RO			
Mirror	MI			
Scale	SC			
Trim	TR			
Extend	EX			
Offset	O			
Fillet	F			
Chamfer	CHA			
Arrayrect (Rectangular Array)	Arrayrect			
Arraypolar (Polar Array)	Arraypolar			

Lesson 7

Create the 2D drawing as shown using the commands listed below.

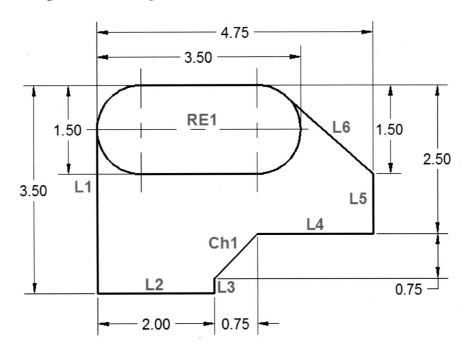

Commands used in this lesson

» Function key "**F12**" (Toggle Dynamic Input on/off)

» Function key "**F8**" (Toggle Ortho on/off)

» Function key "**F3**" (Toggle Osnap <Object Snap> On/off)

» Function key "**F7**" (Grid Display on/off)

» **Line**

» **Chamfer**

» **Rectangle**

Steps	Entities	Command Line Display	Inputs	Comments
1		Type a command	F12 (Function key)	Dynamic Input <On> (Ensure this icon is enabled.)
		MODEL ▦ ▦ ▾ ⊞ ⌐ ⊘ ▾ ✕ ▾ ∠ ▯ ▾ ☰ ▾ ✿ ▾ + ● ⧉ ↗ ☰		
2		Type a command	F8 (Function key)	Ortho <On> (Ensure this icon is enabled.)
		MODEL ▦ ▦ ▾ ⊞ ⌐ ⊘ ▾ ✕ ▾ ∠ ▯ ▾ ☰ ▾ ✿ ▾ + ● ⧉ ↗ ☰		

Steps	Entities	Command Line Display	Inputs	Comments
3		Type a command	F3 (Function key)	Osnap <Off> (Ensure this icon is disabled.)
		MODEL ⊞ ⠿ ▾ ⁺ᴸ ∟ ⟳ ▾ ⤬ ▾ ∠ □ ▾ ▤ ▾ ⚙ ▾ ✛ ● ⯐ ⤢ ☰		
4		Type a command	F7 (Function key)	Grid display <Off> (Ensure this icon is disabled.)
		MODEL ⊞ ⠿ ▾ ⁺ᴸ ∟ ⟳ ▾ ⤬ ▾ ∠ □ ▾ ▤ ▾ ⚙ ▾ ✛ ● ⯐ ⤢ ☰		
5	RE1	Type a command	**rectangle** <Enter>	Enter rectangle command.
6		Specify first corner point or [Chamfer/Elevation/Fillet/Thickness/Width]:	**fillet** <Enter>	Activate fillet option, assign fillet at each corner.
7		Specify fillet radius for rectangles <0>:	**0.75** <Enter>	Enter radius of fillet.
8		Specify first corner point or [Chamfer/Elevation/Fillet/Thickness/Width]:	<Click anywhere within graphic window>	Start from a random point.
9		Specify next point or [Undo]:	**3.5,1.5** <Enter>	Enter X,Y coordinates.
10	L1	Type a command	**line** <Enter>	Enter Line command.
11		Specify first point:	**End** <Enter>	
12		of	<Select left of **RE1**>	
13		Specify next point or [Undo]:	Point downward, type **2.75**<Enter>	Specify line direction & its length.
14	L2	Specify next point or [Undo]:	Point to the right, type **2** <Enter>	
15	L3	Specify next point or [Close/Undo]:	Point upward, type **1** <Enter>	
16	L4	Specify next point or [Close/Undo]:	Point to the right, type **2.75** <Enter>	
17	L5	Specify next point or [Close/Undo]:	Point upward, type **1** <Enter>	
18	L6	Specify next point or [Close/Undo]:	**tan** <Enter>	Activate tangent object snap mode.

Steps	Entities	Command Line Display	Inputs	Comments
19		Specify next point or [Close/ Undo]:	<Select top right of **RE1**>	
20		Specify next point or [Close/ Undo]:	<Enter>	Finish Line command.
21	Ch1	Type a command	**chamfer** <Enter>	Create Chamfer.
22		Select first line or [Undo/ Polyline/Distance/Angle/ Trim/Method/Multiple]:	**d** <Enter>	Set chamfer distance.
23		Specify first chamfer distance <0.0000>:	**0.75** <Enter>	Enter 1st chamfer distance of 0.75.
24		Specify second chamfer distance <0.7500>:	<Enter>	Use the 1st chamfer distance value <0.7500> for the 2nd one.
25		Select first line or [Undo/ Polyline/Distance/Angle/ Trim/Method/Multiple]:	<Select Line **L3**>	
26		Select second line or shift-select to apply corner or [Distance/Angle/Method]:	<Select Line **L4**>	

Lesson 8

Create the 2D drawing as shown using the commands listed below.

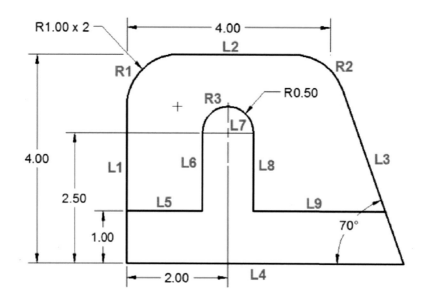

Commands used in this lesson

> » Function key "**F12**" (Toggle Dynamic Input on/off)

> » Function key "**F3**" (Toggle Osnap <Object Snap> on/off)

> » **Line**

> » **UCS**

> » Fillet

> » Circle

> » Trim

> » Delete

Steps	Entities	Command Line Display	Inputs	Comments
1		Type a command	F12 (Function key)	Dynamic Input <On> (Ensure this icon is enabled.)
		MODEL		
2		Type a command	F3 (Function key)	Osnap <On> (Ensure this icon is enabled.)
		MODEL		

Steps	Entities	Command Line Display	Inputs	Comments
3		Type a command	**Osnap** <Enter>	

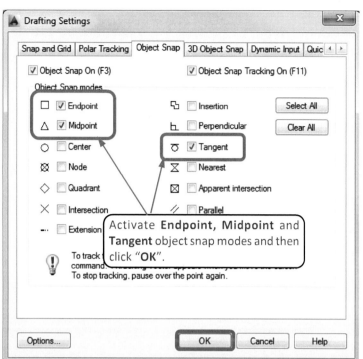

Steps	Entities	Command Line Display	Inputs	Comments
4	L1	Type a command	**line** <Enter>	Enter Line command.
5		Specify first point:	<**Click** anywhere within the graphic window >	Start from a random point.
6		Specify next point or [Undo]:	**0,4** <Enter>	Enter X,Y coordinates.
7	L2	Specify next point or [Undo]:	**4,0** <Enter>	
8	L3	Specify next point or [Close/Undo]:	**5<-70** <Enter>	
9		Specify next point or [Close/Undo]:	<Enter>	Finish Line command.
10	L4	Type a command	**line** <Enter>	Enter Line command.
11		Specify first point:	<Select the end of line **L1**>	

Click here

Steps	Entities	Command Line Display	Inputs	Comments
12		Specify next point or [Undo]:	**6,0** <Enter>	Enter X,Y coordinates

Steps	Entities	Command Line Display	Inputs	Comments
13		Specify next point or [Undo]:	\<Enter\>	Finish Line command.
14		Type a command	UCS \<Enter\>	Set User Coordinate System.
15		Specify origin of UCS:	\<Select the end of line L1\>	Set the end point of L1 as origin.

Click here

16		Specify origin on X-axis or \<accept\>:	\<Enter\>	Accept & finish the UCS command.
17	L5	Type a command	line \<Enter\>	Enter Line command.
18		Specify first point:	0,1 \<ENTER\>	Enter X,Y coordinates.
19		Specify next point or [Undo]:	1.5,0 \<Enter\>	
20	L6	Specify next point or [Undo]:	0,1.5 \<Enter\>	
21	L7	Specify next point or [Close/Undo]:	1,0 \<Enter\>	
22	L8	Specify next point or [Close/Undo]:	0,-1.5 \<Enter\>	
23	L9	Specify next point or [Close/Undo]:	3,0 \<Enter\>	
24		Specify next point or [Close/Undo]:	\<Enter\>	Finish Line command.
25	R1	Type a command	fillet \<Enter\>	Create corner radius.
26		Select first object or [Undo/Polyline/Radius/Trim/Multiple]:	r \<Enter\>	Set fillet radius.
27		Specify fillet radius \<0.0000\>	1 \<Enter\>	Enter radius of 1.
28		Select first object or [Undo/Polyline/Radius/Trim/Multiple]:	\<Select line L1\>	

Steps	Entities	Command Line Display	Inputs	Comments
29		Select second object or shift-select to apply corner or [Radius]:	<Select line **L2**>	
30	R2	Type a command	<Enter>	Repeat last command. (Fillet)
31		Select first object or [Undo/ Polyline/Radius/Trim/ Multiple]:	<Select line **L2**>	Since the radius is already set, it is not necessary to set the radius again.
32		Select second object or shift-select to apply corner or [Radius]:	<Select line **L3**>	
33	R3	Type a command	**circle** <Enter>	Enter circle command.
34		Specify center point for circle or [3P/2P/Ttr (tan tan radius)]:	<Select the middle of line **L7**>	Specify center point for the circle.
35		Specify radius of circle or [Diameter]:	**0.5** <Enter>	Specify radius of circle.
36		Type a command	**trim** <Enter>	Enter Trim command.

Steps	Entities	Command Line Display	Inputs	Comments
37		Select objects or <select all>:	<Select the three lines (**L3, L4, L7**) as shown>	Use these lines as cutting edges to trim other lines and circle.
38		Select objects	<Enter>	Finish selection.
39		Select object to trim or shift-select to extend or [Fence/Crossing/Project/ Edge/eRase/Undo]:	<Select the unwanted portion of the lines **L3, L4 & L9** and the circle **R3** as shown>	Trim away the unwanted lines and circle.
40		Select object to trim or shift-select to extend or [Fence/Crossing/Project/ Edge/eRase/Undo]:	<Enter>	Finish trimming.
41		Type a command	<Click on line **L7**>	Select the line to delete.
42		Type a command	Press <Delete> on the keyboard	Delete the line.

Lesson 9

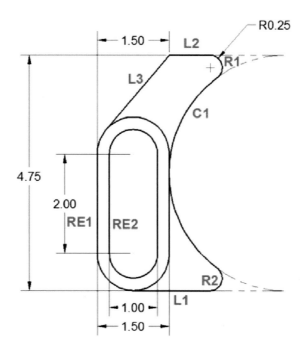

Commands used in this lesson

»   Function key "**F12**" (Toggle Dynamic Input on/off)

»   Function key "**F8**" (Toggle Object Snap on/off)

»   Function key "**F7**" (Toggle Grid Display on/off)

»   **Line**

»   **Rectangle**

»   **Circle**

»   **Offset**

»   **Fillet**

»   **Trim**

Steps	Entities	Command Line Display	Inputs	Comments
1		Type a command	F12 (Function key)	Dynamic Input \<On\> (Ensure its icon is enabled.)
		MODEL ▦ ▦ ▾ ＋▭ ∟ ⊝ ▾ ✗ ▾ ∠ ▫ ▾ ☰ ▾ ✿ ▾ ＋ ● ▯° ⬀ ☰		
2		Type a command	F8 (Function key)	Ortho \<On\> (Ensure its icon is enabled.)
		MODEL ▦ ▦ ▾ ＋▭ ∟ ⊝ ▾ ✗ ▾ ∠ ▫ ▾ ☰ ▾ ✿ ▾ ＋ ● ▯° ⬀ ☰		

Steps		Command Line Display	Inputs	Comments
3		Type a command	F7 (Function key)	Grid display <Off> (Ensure its icon is disabled.)
		MODEL ▦ ▦ ▾ ⊥ └ ⊙ ▾ ⅄ ▾ ∠ ▭ ▾ ≡ ▾ ✿ ▾ ✛ ● ⯀ ◰ ≡		
4	L1	Type a command	**line** <Enter>	Enter Line command.
5		Specify first point:	<**Click** anywhere within graphic window>	Start from a random point.
6		Specify next point or [Undo]:	Point to the right, type **5**<Enter>	Specify line direction & its length.
7		Specify next point or [Undo]:	<Enter>	Finish Line command.
8	RE1	Type a command	**rectangle** <Enter>	Enter rectangle command.
9		Specify first corner point or [Chamfer/Elevation/Fillet/Thickness/Width]:	**fillet** <Enter>	Assign fillet at each corner.
10		Specify fillet raduis for rectangles <0>:	**0.75** <Enter>	Enter radius of fillet.
11		Specify first corner point or [Chamfer/Elevation/Fillet/Thickness/Width]:	**end** <Enter>	Activate end point snap.
12		of	<**Select** left end of Line **L1**>	 Endpoint
12		Specify next point or [Undo]:	**1.5,3.5** <Enter>	Enter X,Y coordinates.
13	L2	Type a command	**offset** <Enter>	Enter offset command.
14		Specify offset distance or [Through/Erase/Layer] <Through>:	**4.75** <Enter>	Enter distance between edges.
15		Select object to offset or [Exit/Undo] <Exit> :	<**Select** Line **L1**>	
16		Specify point on side to offset or [Exit/Multiple/Undo] <Exit>:	<**Click** anywhere above Line **L1**>	
17		Select object to offset or [Exit/Undo] <Exit> :	<Enter>	Finish Offset command.
18	RE2	Type a command	<Enter>	Repeat last command (offset).
19		Specify offset distance or [Through/Erase/Layer] <Through>:	**0.25** <Enter>	Enter distance between edges.

Steps		Command Line Display	Inputs	Comments
20		Select object to offset or [Exit/Undo] <Exit> :	<Select Rectangle **RE1**>	
21		Specify point on side to offset or [Exit/Multiple/ Undo] <Exit>:	<**Click** anywhere inside RE1>	
22		Select object to offset or [Exit/Undo] <Exit> :	<Enter>	Finish Offset command.
23	L3	Type a command	**line** <Enter>	Enter Line command.
24		Specify first point:	**tan** <Enter>	Activate tangent snap.
25		To	<Select top left portion of **RE1**>	
26		Specify next point or [Undo]:	@3<50	
27		Specify next point or [Close/ Undo]:	<Enter>	Finish Line command.
28	C1	Type a command	**Circle** <Enter>	Enter Circle command.
29		Specify center point for circle or [3P/2P/Ttr (tan tan radius)]:	**3P** <Enter>	Activate "3 points" option.
30		Specify first point on circle:	**tan** <Enter>	Activate tangent snap.
31		to	<Select Line L1>	

Steps	Command Line Display	Inputs	Comments
32	Specify second point on circle:	**tan** <Enter>	
33	to	<Select right edge of Rectangle RE1 >	
34	Specify third point on circle:	**tan** <Enter>	
35	to	<Select Line L2>	
36	Type a command	**trim** <Enter>	Enter Trim command.
37	Select objects or <select all>:	<Enter>	Use all edges as cutting edges to trim each other.
38	[Fence/Crossing/Project/ Edge/Erase/Undo]:	<Select unwanted portions of Lines **L1, L2, L3** & Circle **C1** as shown>	Trim away the unwanted lines and circle.

These two selection are optional because fillet command will trim them.

Steps	Command Line Display	Inputs	Comments
39	[Fence/Crossing/Project/ Edge/Erase/Undo]:	<Enter>	Finish trim command.

Steps		Command Line Display	Inputs	Comments
40	R1	Type a command	**fillet** \<Enter\>	Create corner radius.
41		Select first object or [Undo/Polyline/Radius/Trim/Multiple]:	**r** \<Enter\>	Set fillet radius.
42		Specify fillet radius \<0.0000\>	**0.25** \<Enter\>	Enter radius of 0.25.
43		Select first object or [Undo/Polyline/Radius/Trim/Multiple]:	\<Select line **L1**\>	
		Select second object or shift-select to apply corner or [Radius]:	\<Select Circle **C1**\>	
44	R2	Type a command	\<Enter\>	Repeat last command (Fillet).
45		Select first object or [Undo/Polyline/Radius/Trim/Multiple]:	\<Select line **L2**\>	Since the radius is already set, it is not necessary to set the radius again.
		Select second object or shift-select to apply corner or [Radius]:	\<Select line **C1**\>	

Exercise 10.1

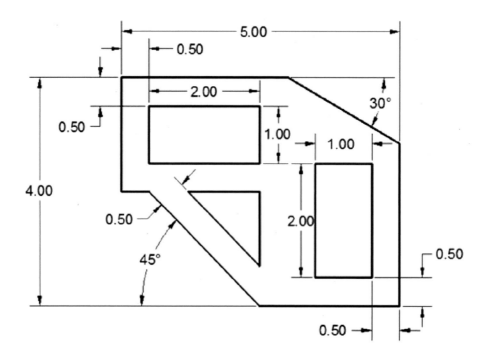

Exercise 10.2

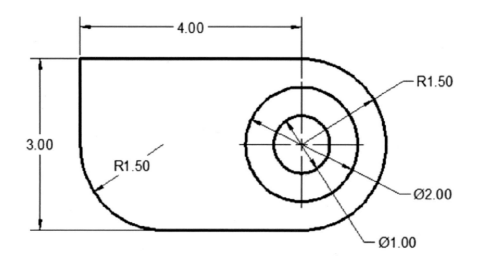

Exercise 10.3

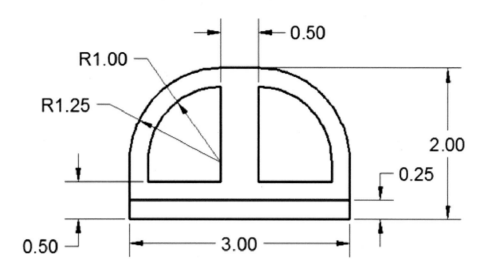

Exercise 10.4

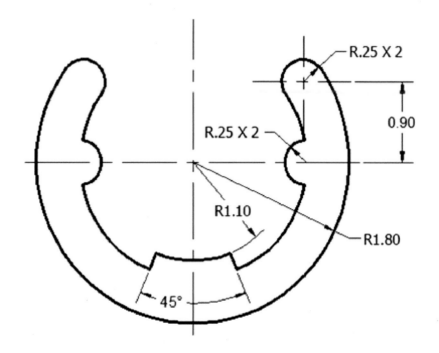

Exercise 10.5

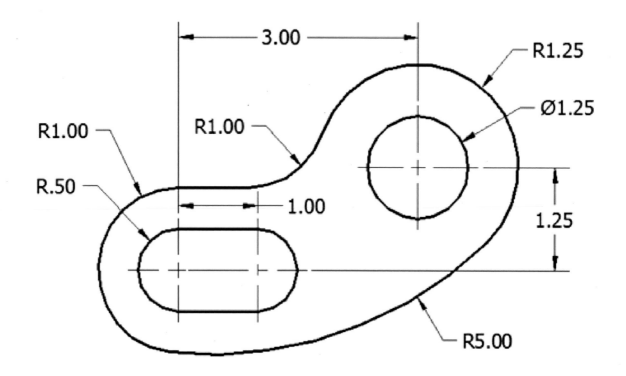

Exercise 10.6

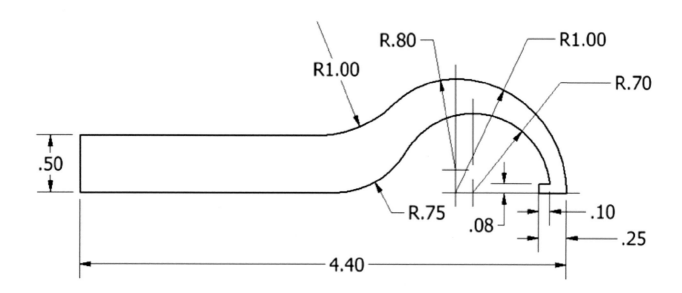

Exercise 10.7

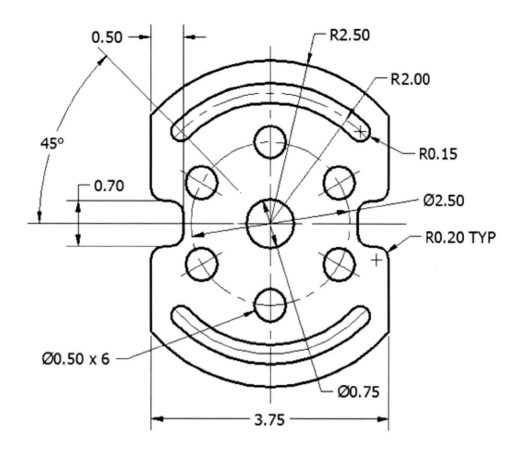

Exercise 10.8

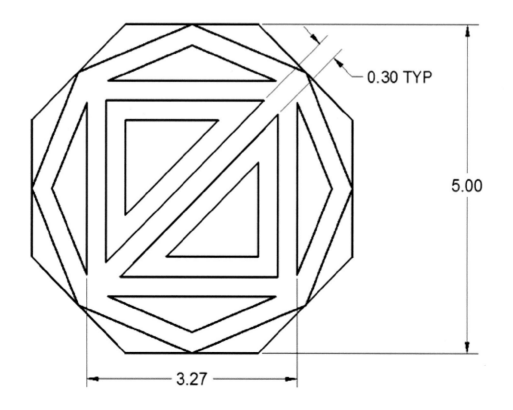

DIMENSIONING AND TOLERANCING IN AUTOCAD

The introduction of dimensioning and tolerancing for technical drawings was covered in Chapter 3. In this chapter, we will focus on the applications of dimension commands. The dimension commands are grouped in the Annotation panel of the Home tab as shown in Figure 11.1 or the Dimensions panel of the Annotate tab as shown in Figure 11.2. The commands are further organized by their types in which their functions are described visually by their icons as shown in Figure 11.3.

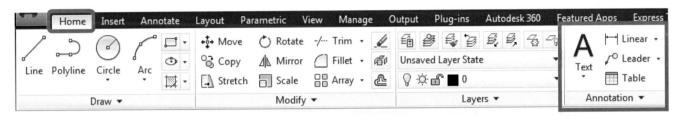

FIGURE 11.1: Annotation panel

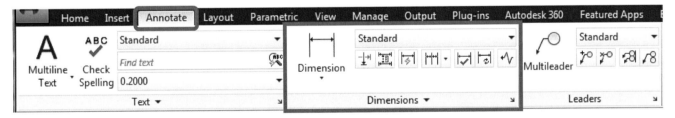

FIGURE 11.2: Dimensions panel

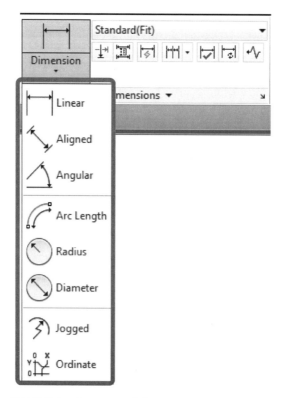

FIGURE 11.3: Types of dimension commands

11.1 EDITING DIMENSION STYLE

A dimension style contains many parameters such as dimension lines, extension lines, arrow size, text height, precision, and tolerances which all need to be considered when applying dimensions in AutoCAD. This is important because the default setting of the dimension style may not be suitable for all drawing sizes and dimensions. Figure 11.4 shows seven important parameters for a typical dimension in AutoCAD.

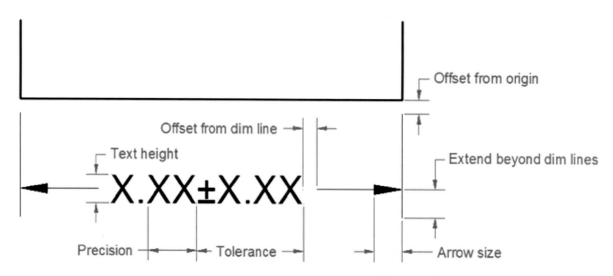

FIGURE 11.4: Parameters for a typical dimension.

11.1.1 How to edit the current Dimension Style

1. Enable the Dimension Style Manager dialog box by clicking on the arrow at the lower right corner of the Dimensions panel within the Annotate tab or by entering **DIMSTYLE** in the Command Line Window.

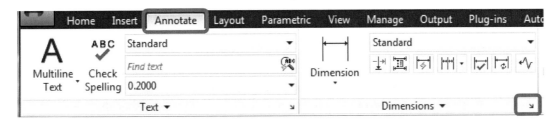

2. Select the dimension style (Standard) on the left of the dialog box and click "**Modify**".

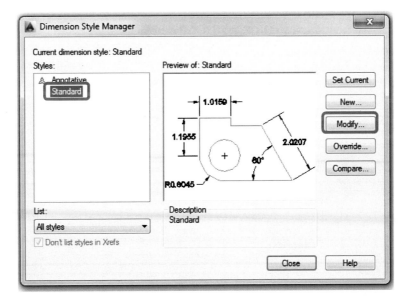

a. On the <u>Lines tab,</u> use Figure 11.4 as reference and modify the values of the **Extend Beyond dim lines** and the **Offset from origin**.

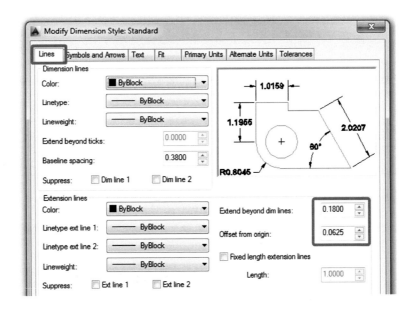

b. On the <u>Symbols and Arrows tab</u>, use Figure 11.4 as reference and modify the value of the **Arrow size**.

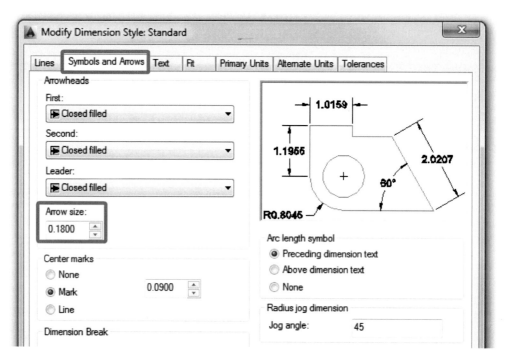

c. On the <u>Text tab</u>, use Figure 11.4 as reference and modify the values of the **Text height** and **Offset from dim line**.

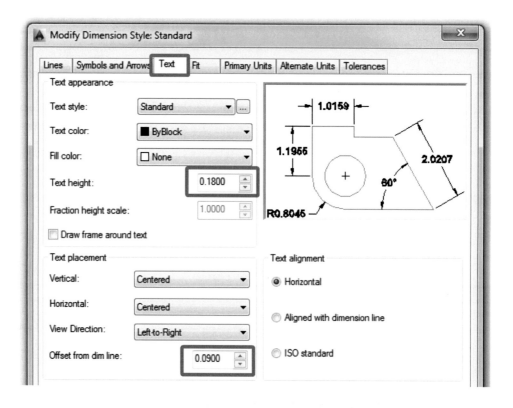

d.   On the <u>Primary Units tab</u>, use Figure 11.4 as reference and modify the settings of the **Unit format** and **Precision**.

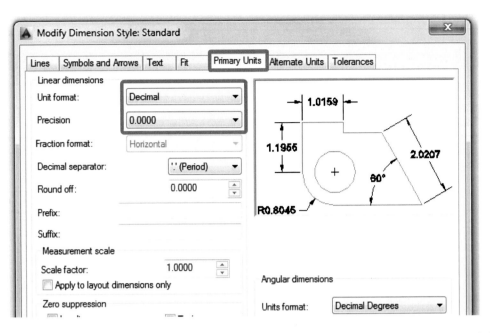

e.   On the <u>Tolerances tab</u>, use Section 3.4.2 as reference and modify the settings of the Tolerance format including **Method** and **Precision** and the values of the **Upper value, Lower value,** and **Scaling for height**.

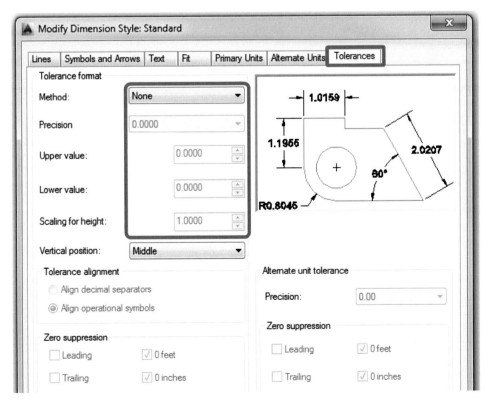

3.   Click "**OK**" after all settings and values are modified accordingly.

   Note: In general, when you change the dimension parameters, use the same scale factor for all the values.

11.1.2 How to create a new Dimension Style

1. Enable the Dimension Style Manager dialog box by clicking on the arrow at the lower right corner of the Dimensions panel or by entering **DIMSTYLE** in the Command Line Window.

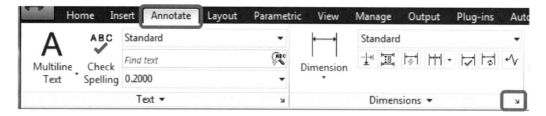

2. Click "**New**" on the dialog box.

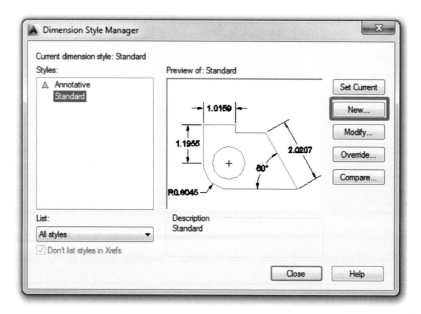

3. Enter the New Style Name (e.g. style 1) in the Create New Dimension Style dialog box and click "**Continue**".

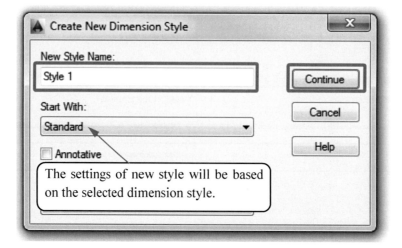

4. Modify the new dimension style using the method introduced previously and click "**OK**" to accept the settings.

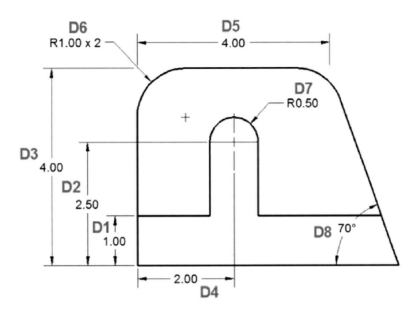

Commands used in this lesson

» Function key "**F3**" (Toggle Osnap <Object Snap> on/off)

» **Osnap**

» **Linear dimension** | Linear

» Radius dimension ◯ Radius

» Angular dimension △ Angular

Open the drawing created in Lesson 8.

Steps	Entities	Command Line Display	Inputs	Comments
1		Type a command	F3 (Function key)	Osnap <On> (Ensure this icon is enabled.)
		MODEL ▦ ▦ ▾ ⁺ ∟ ↻ ▾ ⤫ ▾ ◿ ▣ ▾ ☰ ▾ ✿ ▾ ✛ ● ⬗ ↗ ☰		
2		Type a command	**Osnap** <Enter>	

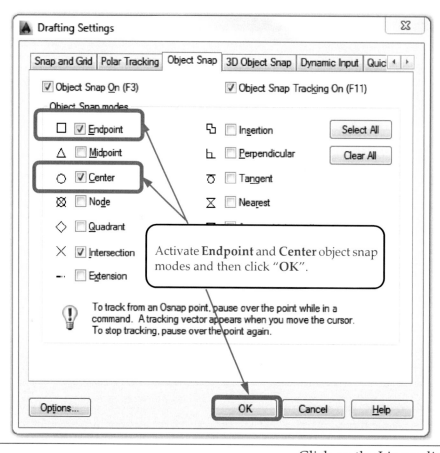

3	D1	Type a command	⊢—⊣ Linear	Click on the Linear dimension command located in the Annotation tab.
4		Specify first extension line origin or <select object>:	<Click on the following steps>	
5	D2	Type a command	<Enter>	Repeat Linear dimension command.
6		Specify first extension line origin or <select object>:	<Click on the following steps>	
7	D3	Type a command	<Enter>	Repeat Linear dimension command.

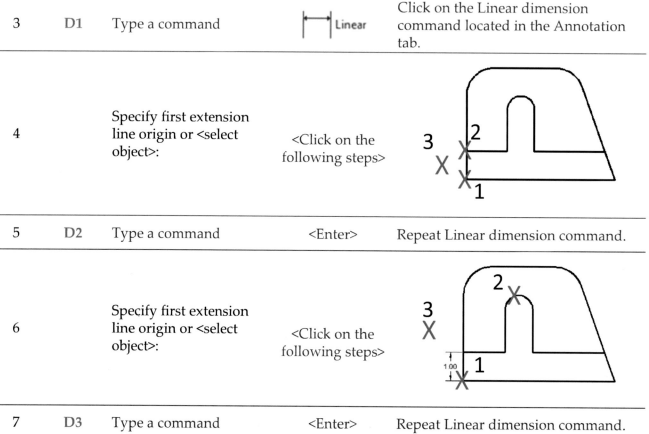

Steps	Entities	Command Line Display	Inputs	Comments
8		Specify first extension line origin or <select object>:	**int** <Enter>	Activate intersection snap.
9		of	<Click on the following steps>	
10		Specify second extension line origin:	<Click on the following steps>	
11	D4	Type a command	<Enter>	Repeat Linear dimension command.
12		Specify first extension line origin or <select object>:	<Click on the following steps>	
13	D5	Type a command	<Enter>	Repeat Linear dimension command.
14		Specify first extension line origin or <select object>:	**int** <Enter>	
15		of	<Click on the following steps>	

Steps	Entities	Command Line Display	Inputs	Comments
16		Specify second extension line origin:	int <Enter>	
17		of	\<Click on the following steps\>	
18	D6	Type a command	Radius	Click on the Radius dimension command located in the Annotation tab.
19		Select arc or circle:	\<Click on the following steps\>	
20		Type a command	\<Double Click on the radius dimension\>	Edit the text by double clicking the dimension.
21			add "x 2" after the dimension	Note: press the right arrow key on the keyboard to ensure the cursor is on the right of the dimension.
22	D7	Type a command	\<Enter\>	Repeat Radius dimension command.
23		Select arc or circle:	\<Click on the following steps\>	

Steps	Entities	Command Line Display	Inputs	Comments
24	D8	Type a command	Angular	Click on the Angular dimension command located in the Annotation tab.
25		Select arc, circle, line, or <specify vertex>:	<Click on the following steps>	

Exercises - Chapter 11

Exercise 11.1 Use AutoCAD to create three orthographic views for Exercise 2.1.

Exercise 11.2 Use AutoCAD to create three orthographic views for Exercise 2.3.

Exercise 11.3 Use AutoCAD to create three orthographic views for Exercise 2.5.

Exercise 11.4 Use AutoCAD to create three orthographic views for Exercise 2.7.

Exercise 11.5 Use AutoCAD to create three orthographic views for Exercise 2.9.

Exercise 11.6 Use AutoCAD to create three orthographic views and a section view for Exercise 4.1.

Exercise 11.7 Use AutoCAD to create three orthographic views and a section view for Exercise 4.2.

Exercise 11.8 Use AutoCAD to create three orthographic views and a section view for Exercise 4.3.

LINE TYPES AND LAYERS

The method of constructing and modifying geometries as well as proper dimensioning techniques in AutoCAD were discussed in the previous chapters. This chapter focuses mainly on layers and other object properties such as linetypes and colors.

12.1 LINETYPES AND COLORS

Linetypes and their functions were discussed in Chapter 1. This section shows the required steps to modify the current line type and color in AutoCAD to the desired ones.

12.1.1 How to change the linetype of an existing object(s)

1. Load existing linetypes from the program database.

    a. Enable the Linetype Manager dialog box by selecting "**Other...**" from the Properties panel or by entering **LINETYPE** in the Command Line Window.

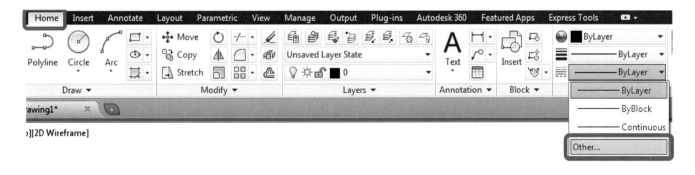

b.   Click "**Load**" on the dialog box.

c.   Browse the Load or Reload Linetypes dialog box, select the proper linetype for your applications and click "**OK**".

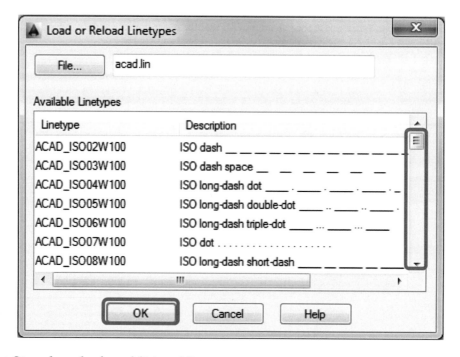

d.   Repeat Steps b and c for additional linetypes.

e.   Click "**OK**" on the Linetype Manager dialog box.

2.   Change the linetype of an existing object(s).

a.   Select the object(s) from the graphics window.

b.   Select the linetype from the Properties panel.

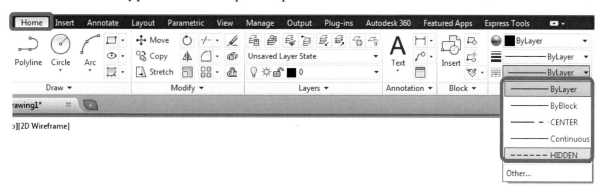

3.   Change the linetype scale if necessary. (e.g. If centerlines do not show proper long and short line pattern or if hidden lines seem like continuous lines.)

a.   Enter **LTSCALE** in the Command Line Window.

b.   Enter **new linetype scale factor** in the Command Line Window. (The scale factor should be larger than, equal to, or smaller than 1.)

12.2 LAYERS

Layers in AutoCAD work similar to transparent overlays in paper-based drafting. The best use of layers is to organize a group of objects based on their functions, locations, line types, colors, or line thicknesses. By selectively turning the layers on and off, objects within a complex drawing can be selectively displayed and plotted.

Layers can be created before or after the drawing is completed or during the geometry construction. However, in general, drawings should be constructed on the original layer as much as possible before assigning portions of the drawing into different layers.

12.2.1 Layer command and its functions

Figure 12.1 shows the Layer Properties Manager dialog box. Layers can be added, deleted, and renamed in this dialog box. Properties of the layer can also be assigned and modified in this dialog box. The property options shown in Figure 12.1 are listed and explained in the following.

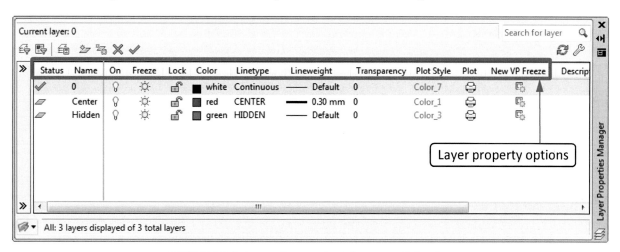

FIGURE 12.1: Layer Properties Manager dialog box

Status – The ✔ icon in the status column indicates the selected layer is active.

On – Layers can be turned on ◯ or off ◯ for visualization.

Name – Displays the name of the layers.

Freeze – Objects on frozen layers are not displayed, plotted, hidden, or regenerated.

Lock – Objects on a locked layer cannot be modified.

Color – Displays the color of the objects associated with the **selected** layers.

Linetype – Displays the linetype associated with the **selected** layers.

Lineweight – Displays the lineweight associated with the **selected** layers.

Transparency - Controls the transparency of all objects on the selected layers.

Plot Style – Displays the plot style associated with the **selected** layers.

Plot – Layers can be included 🖨 or excluded 🖨 for plotting.

12.2.2 How to assign an object(s) into a different layer

1. Create new layers with specific properties
    a. Enable the Layer Properties Manager dialog box by selecting "**Layer properties**" 📚 from the Layers panel or by entering **LAYER** in the Command line.
    b. Select "**New Layer**" 📑 from the dialog box.
    c. Right click on the new layer name, select "**Rename Layer**" and enter a new name for the layer. (In this demonstration, create a Layer named Center and another Layer named Hidden.)

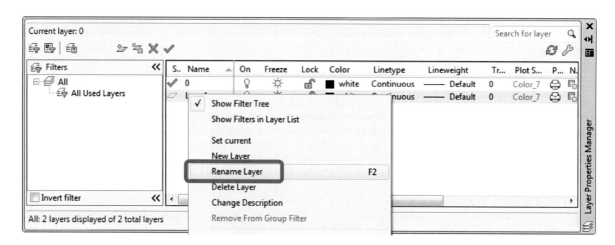

    d. Repeat steps b and c for additional layers.

e. Click on Color, Linetype, and Lineweight of each layer to assign the specific properties of the layer.

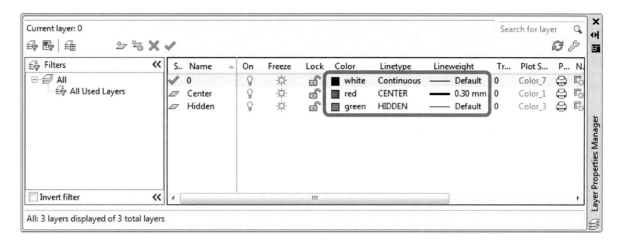

2. Assign an existing object(s) into a different layer.

    a. Select the object(s) from the graphics window.

    b. Select the layer from the layer panel.

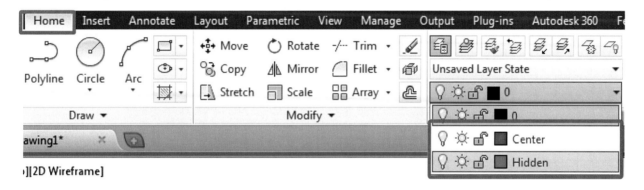

12.3 PROPERTIES

Object properties such as linetype, color, and layer can be customized individually or as a group of objects. The general panel in the Properties dialog box shown in Figure 12.2 displays the basic properties of an object or a group of objects.

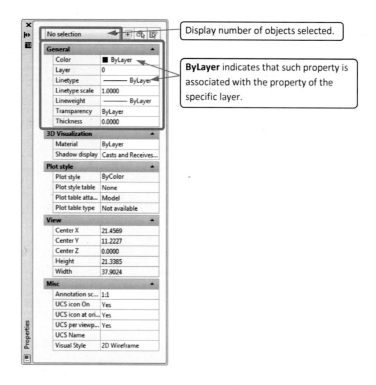

FIGURE 12.2: Properties dialog box

12.3.1 How to assign different properties to an object(s)

1. Enable the Properties dialog box by clicking on the arrow at the lower right corner of the properties panel within the Home tab or by entering **PROPERTIES** in the Command line.

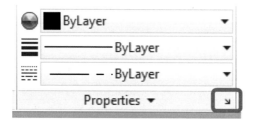

2. Select the object(s) from the graphics window.

3. Click on the property settings to assign the desired properties.

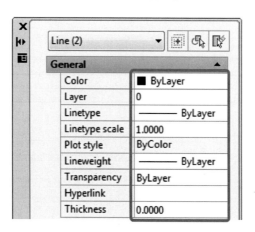